Making MUSIC Your BUSINESS

A GUIDE FOR YOUNG MUSICIANS

By David Ellefson

Miller Freeman Books

San Francisco

Published by Miller Freeman Books
600 Harrison Street, San Francisco, CA 94107
Publishers of *Guitar Player*, *Bass Player*, and *Keyboard* magazines

un Miller Freeman
A United News & Media company

Distributed to the book trade in the U.S. and Canada by Publishers Group West, P.O. Box 8843, Emeryville, CA 94662

Distributed to the music trade in the U.S. and Canada by Hal Leonard Publishing, P.O. Box 13819, Milwaukee, WI 53213

Design: Greene Design
Production Editor/Layout: Jan Hughes
Editor: Jim Roberts
Cover Photo: Gene Kirkland
Back Cover Photo: Pete Cronin

Library of Congress Cataloging in Publication Data:
Ellefson, David.   1964–
        Making music your business : a guide for young musicians / by
        David Ellefson.
                p.   cm.
        ISBN 0-87930-460-X (alk. paper)
        1. Popular music—Vocational guidance. 2. Music trade.
I. Title.
ML3795.E43   1997   ·   97-9673
780'.23'73 — dc21   CIP
                                                         MN

ISBN 0-87930-460-X

Printed in the United States of America
97 98 99 00 01 02   5 4 3 2 1

TABLE OF CONTENTS

PART ONE: IN THE BEGINNING

PART TWO: THE TEAM

PART THREE: RECORDING

PART FOUR: TRAVELING

PART FIVE: GEAR & MORE

PART SIX: IN CLOSING

APPENDIX

 OREWORD

THE IDEA FOR THIS BOOK CAME TO ME DURING THE recording of the Megadeth album *Youthanasia*, and through every phase of that album-and-tour cycle, I found myself inspired to write chapters pertaining to the events that were happening around me. My aim was not to write a how-to book, strictly speaking, but rather to share some insights and experiences that might aid aspiring artists who wish to develop careers in the mad enterprise we call the "music industry."

Throughout the *Youthanasia* tour, I was posting daily updates from the road on the Megadeth Arizona World Wide Web site on a page called "The Obituary." Toward the end of the tour, I received an e-mail from Jim Roberts of *Bass Player*, asking me if I would like to write for the magazine. I was honored by the invitation to contribute to such a prestigious and respected magazine, and I accepted the offer. As we talked about my new column, I told Jim about this book, and he suggested I contact the book division of the magazine's publisher, Miller Freeman, Inc. A short while later, we agreed on a deal to publish the book.

In addition to writing about my own experiences, I interviewed a number of other artists hoping their insights would help to expand some of the points I was making. As you'll notice, all of the artists I spoke with have put in years and years of hard work to achieve their success. I found this to be very inspiring, especially since we live in an age of sound bites where you can be here today and gone later today if you play by everyone else's rules!

Many people contributed to this book. I especially want to thank my wife, Julie, for her painstaking efforts in helping me to edit the original manuscript. I'd also like to thank my son, Roman; my mother, Frances; my late father, Gordon; and my brother, Eliot. Thanks also to Jim Roberts, Matt Kelsey, Jan Hughes, Dave Mustaine, Marty Friedman, Nick Menza, Mike Renault, Bud Prager, Brett Merritt, Gene Kirkland, Pete Cronin, Mike Varney, Val Janes, Suzan Crane, Billy Sheehan, Will Lee, Chrissie Hynde, Norma Bishop and GailForce Management, Slash, Tom Maher, Tori Amos, Donna Jaffe, Spivak Entertainment, Ken Hensley, Andy West, Dave Pomeroy, Joey Ramone, Ira Lippy, Larry Wallack, Bob Mothersbaugh, Bob Timmons, Audrey Strahl, Gina Rainville, Carla White, Joe Dicioccio, EMI Music Publishing, Evelyn Buckstein and BMI, Hendrik Huigen, Andy Somers, Dave Downey, Doug Thaler, Skip Rickert, Jeff Yonker, Jerry Giefer, and Greg Carlson. This list could never really be complete because of the many people who have helped me in my musical career over the last 20 years. Thank you for your enthusiasm and for fueling my own spirit and passion for music.

God Bless,

David Ellefson

PART ONE

IN THE BEGINNING

UCKLE UP FOR SAFETY

CONSIDERING THE NUMBER OF PEOPLE WHO HAVE TAKEN
a shot at becoming professional musicians, I think I'm very
fortunate to have reached the level of success I've achieved in
my career. My journey has taken me from small clubs in the
Midwest to the finest recording studios and largest concert
arenas in the world. This experience has been invaluable, and
it's taught me many things I could not have learned in any
classroom. I've learned a lot about *music,* and I've learned a
lot about the *music business.* Both of these are endless
subjects, and sharpening the survival skills you need to
succeed in the music business is every bit as important as
becoming a good musician. That's what this book is about.

Succeeding in music really boils down to common sense
and perseverance. In most cases, success comes to those who
choose the line of work they truly love and in turn love what
they do. When I was a young, enthusiastic musician, many
people scoffed when I said I was going to make a living playing music—but I knew it was my destiny. So, after I graduated
from high school, I chose not to sentence myself to the
standard four years of college and instead went for an educa-
tion in the music business—the school of hard knocks. (While
many are worthy of diplomas in this school, no one has
handed them out yet!)

I was 18 years old when I left my hometown in Minnesota

and headed for Los Angeles. I set out on my journey with three friends, a little bit of cash, and my musical equipment. I had only one contact in Hollywood, and she was the landlady who was reserving an apartment for me when I arrived. At this point I had played music professionally (which means someone had actually paid me to play) for about five years, and I thought I had a pretty good chance of getting a gig of some sort. I soon learned otherwise, and being a small-town boy in "Hollyweird" freaked me out at first. I knew I was in for some serious

IN MOST CASES, SUCCESS COMES TO THOSE WHO CHOOSE THE LINE OF WORK THEY TRULY LOVE AND IN TURN LOVE WHAT THEY DO.

growing pains. Fortunately, I soon hooked up with others who were also strongly motivated to succeed. One thing led to another, and before long I began to see many of my dreams materialize.

I quickly realized there were many starving artists in L.A. who had visions for their careers that were quite different from mine. I also realized that in spite of the many schools, books, and video cassettes that teach you how to play music, there didn't seem to be a classroom that taught the pros and cons of the music business. In that respect, we musicians are pretty much on our own, and we often encounter serious bumps and bruises as we find our way in this volatile industry. Most of the valuable lessons I've learned have been through trial and error, and I'm often asked about these lessons by aspiring musicians who need help to get to the next level of their careers. I think it's in our best interest to help and support each other whenever we can, and this book is a way for me to respond to many of these questions.

Some people say luck is a key ingredient of success, and that may be true. But I also believe the harder a person works, the luckier he becomes. I'm convinced that our chances for success are greatly increased by hard work and the pursuit of more and more knowledge. My aim here is to impart some of the wisdom I've acquired along the way. A note before I plunge in: Many of the references in this book are male in gender. For reasons of simplicity (and, hopefully, good grammar), I often say "he" rather than "he or she." This is not meant to be chauvinistic but was done just for simplicity and continuity throughout the book. Believe me, the ideas, philosophies, and experiences shared in this book can apply to *anyone*, regardless of sex, age, race, species, or musical taste.

Bearing that in mind, I wish you all the best in your endeavors and remember: Buckle up for safety, because this is the ride of a lifetime!

OUR CHANCES FOR SUCCESS ARE GREATLY INCREASED BY HARD WORK AND THE PURSUIT OF MORE KNOWLEDGE. HERE, DAVID ELLEFSON DOING WHAT HE DOES BEST: PLAYING BASS FOR MEGADETH.

ETTING STARTED

I WILL ALWAYS REMEMBER A SAYING I HEARD YEARS AGO: Musicians must eat crow, smile, and ask for more. After playing in many short-lived bands early in my career, I realized that my quest for the big time was not going to be an easy one—and that perhaps there was some truth to this quote!

The early stages of building a musical career can be a very trying time, and they may teach you more about your breaking point than you care to know. It's quite a juggling act to write, rehearse, and record your music while trying to learn the business aspect of music and stay sane. (Sanity is, of course, an option in the music industry.)

When talking with aspiring players, I'm often asked how they can get started in the music business. Well, I've got to be honest with you—when I started out, the whole thing seemed like a big mystery to me, too. So the first thing I say is: "You don't wake up one day and realize you've made it." It doesn't just happen; you must work diligently and hope your talent and persistence (plus a little luck) will eventually lead to the breaks that are needed to have a professional music career.

If you're searching for the secret to success, I suggest you stop right now and realize there's no such thing. In fact, all I can really do in this book is share my experiences—as well as those of some of my fellow professionals—in the hope that you will learn enough to be able to create your own niche in the world of

IF YOU'RE ALREADY IN A BAND AND MAK-
ING LIVE PERFORMANCES, IT'S CRUCIAL
TO BE ON THE SCENE AND REGULARLY
NETWORKING THROUGH WORD OF MOUTH.
PICTURED HERE, DAVID ELLEFSON IN HIS
EARLY DAYS: TOP, AGE 18, MINNESOTA;
BOTTOM, AGE 16, IOWA.

"Good Times"
CD Release Party!

heyday RECORDS

Chris Cacav...
& Junk Yard Love
Viva Satur...
featuring Steven Roba...
...t Thor...
...the Family Je...
...y Sk...
...e...
...ha...

mk-ULTRA
and
BrAcKeT

HEINZ TOMATO KETCHUP

mk-ULTRA (formerly Cylinder) CD Release Party!

9:30 P.M.

100% ...GE... WORLD MIND CON...

WEDNESDAY
OCTOBER 27

Bottom of the Hill
1722 Seventeenth Street

COLE MARQUIS
BOXERDOG

CHAMELEON
EARLY SHOW
5PM

...DAY MARCH 8

cyl
in
der
STIMMIES
CHALK CIRCLE

p a r a d i s e   l o u n g e

SEEK OUT ALL PERFORMANCE OPPORTUNITIES; CONSIDER PLAYING PARTIES, DANCES, AND NIGHTCLUBS TO BE BASIC TRAINING. THESE GIGS ARE GREAT JUMPING-OFF POINTS FOR TIGHTENING UP YOUR ACT.

14

music. So if anyone tells you he has it all figured out, I suggest you walk away and save yourself from an earful of B.S.

While being in the right place at the right time can be extremely helpful, I feel that individuality, charisma, and integrity are the real keys to any artist's survival. Hey, I'd love to spell out a magical plan for overnight success, but there just doesn't seem to be one. The good news is that most of us use a similar approach in piecing together the essentials of a music career, and those essentials are what I've tried to put in this book.

For starters, put things in perspective and figure out what it is you want from playing music. Do you want to make music a full-time career, or is it just a leisure pastime reserved for special occasions? Then ask yourself how much you're willing to sacrifice in order to achieve your goal. The answers to these questions may seem obvious, but you'd be surprised to know how many musicians have become distracted by their lifestyles and completely lost sight of their original goals. By establishing a game plan, you can focus your energies and not squander valuable time and money.

In the early stages of your career, a few simple steps will get you off to a good start. First things first: Write your own music. Second, seek out all performance opportunities; consider playing parties, dances, and nightclubs to be basic training. These gigs are great jumping-off points for tightening up your act and learning to read an audience's response.

If you're already in a band and making live performances, it's crucial to be on the scene and regularly networking through word of mouth. Believe it or not, this can be just as important as your actual talent. If you think someone will knock on your door one day and invite you to become rich and famous, you'd better think again. In Minnesota, where I grew up, my earliest bands spent a great deal of time hanging up flyers in our hometown and the neighboring cities. We played all the usual high school dances and keg parties, and we took slots opening for established acts, hoping that someone would "discover" us. We didn't become instantly successful, but I learned that the more you make your presence known through your own efforts, the more you improve your chances of succeeding.

This leads us to the next step: putting together a team of people who will help to further your career. A reliable team of professional managers and agents can take your musical vision to new heights. My experience has been that without the guidance of these key people, it's virtually impossible to be a real contender in the music business.

Young musicians are especially vulnerable to the "sharks" who feed on naïveté. I suggest meeting with as many managers, agents, and record-label executives as possible—find out what they're about and what they have to offer. There's nothing wrong with absorbing as much information as possible, but before you sign any long-term agreements with anyone, you must be very clear on how the vision of these people is going to fit in with yours.

One good way to investigate managers, booking agents, and record companies is to talk with artists who have already worked with them. It may be worthwhile to set up a showcase and invite as many of these people to the performance as possible. This can be done either publicly in a nightclub or privately at a sound stage. A showcase is a great way to create a "buzz" about your act—but if you live in a remote part of the world, it may mean considerable travel and expense. It might be better to send a representative of your group to a major music metropolis to generate interest within the industry. That way, you can develop local contacts—and it's a whole lot cheaper than moving the whole band!

TEAMWORK

TEAMWORK IS THE FOUNDATION FOR SUCCESS IN ALL successful organizations. It's probably mentioned most often in the world of sports—it's hard to listen to a sports broadcast without hearing a discussion of team "chemistry" or some comments about how the sum of the parts is greater than the individuals. Consider the position of a football quarterback: He's often regarded as the star player, but he can't win the games by himself. The quarterback relies on the expertise of the coaching staff and the efforts of the linemen, receivers, and other players. All these components working together are what makes a football team successful. By working together as a team, everyone shares in the efforts and the rewards.

There are many similarities between sports and music. In the music business teamwork operates at many levels, some of which may not be obvious. The members of a band must get along with each other musically and personally in order to survive, and they must also have good working relationships with their manager, agent, record company reps, and road personnel. All of these people together make up your musical team.

The same principle applies for session players, too. Prominent session bassist Dave Pomeroy says the team mentality is a strong factor in Nashville, where he does

THE MEMBERS OF A BAND MUST GET ALONG
WITH EACH OTHER MUSICALLY AND PERSON-
ALLY IN ORDER TO SURVIVE. PICTURED
HERE: SOUNDGARDEN.

most of his work. "As the leader of a session, it's important to be aware of the fine line between offering helpful direction and being a control freak," says Dave. "There are few things more satisfying than a job well done, especially when the combined efforts of a number of people result in far more than you could have done yourself."

Some people refuse to be team players, and most of them suffer the consequences sooner or later. An artist with a raging, out-of-control ego may think that if it weren't for him, nothing would matter—so whatever he says goes, despite other opinions. He's likely to learn otherwise. Arrogance and an over-inflated sense of self-importance are rarely conducive to a team mentality. These qualities don't contribute to the success of a team—and they'll alienate you from people faster than a speeding bullet.

How do you start to piece together the members of your team? First, every group needs a leader. Someone needs to be accountable for the project, unless you're a solo artist (in which case you've pretty much designated yourself as your own leader). With one key person at the helm, it's easier to put the team together and spell out each member's role right from the beginning. Let's face it—in most cases, one person (possibly two) has the vision and foresight to guide the project. It's important to consider feedback from everyone in the group, but having a leader will help the operation to run more efficiently.

Allow me to share a simple yet important piece of business etiquette: It's to your advantage to align the members of your team to work toward the common goal of the organization. In other words, share the work and you will all share the wealth. Let everyone do the job he was hired to do. This helps to dispel mutiny, which may manifest itself in the form of private agendas. Once these agendas get started, they can quickly undermine the team's well being. But if everyone feels he's getting a fair deal, then everyone will be motivated to help achieve the team's overall success. Remember, as the team succeeds, so do all the individuals.

Of course, not all working relationships turn out to be as successful as we'd like them to be. Sometimes a change is necessary. Having had the experience (more than once), I dislike being in a situation where there's a "revolving door" for employees. But if someone's motives have strayed, or if he's lost the passion for the job, a change may be the best course of action. For obvious reasons, the most direct and honest approach is usually best for everyone involved. That's why it's important to be clear about job descriptions. It's always good business practice to establish comfortable boundaries within the team. Teamwork requires compromise and commitment— but never forget that there is strength in numbers.

AS THE TEAM SUCCEEDS, SO DO THE INDIVIDUALS.

Creating a demand for yourself as a musician is a complicated process that requires you to evaluate yourself and your surroundings as objectively as possible. It's important to keep the big picture in mind, with as few prior assumptions as possible. Think about what you have to offer a potential employer or collaborator, and try to identify your strengths and unique characteristics. It's important to think about your weak points, too, and decide how to improve or minimize them. Be prepared to reevaluate your circumstances regularly—life changes constantly.

—Dave Pomeroy

NASHVILLE STUDIO BASSIST

PART TWO

THE TEAM

PERSONAL MANAGEMENT

COMPETENT ARTIST MANAGEMENT IS ESSENTIAL TO YOUR career. As Bob Mothersbaugh of Devo recalls, "Before we made our first record, we had a lot of interest from people like David Bowie and Iggy Pop, so Warner Bros. got in touch and wanted to sign us. They then asked us to get a manager, because they didn't like dealing with us directly." If you hope to be successful, you will need career guidance through management.

There are different types of managers: personal managers, business managers, tour managers, production managers, and others. My primary focus in this chapter is on personal management. This is a very loose and broad term because of the variety of tasks a personal manager often handles. Generally referred to simply as "the manager," he is the artist's primary representative. It's his job to look after the day-to-day affairs of the artists he works with; these duties include working with attorneys, record labels, producers, merchandisers, and booking agents as well as hiring tour personnel.

Along with your attorney, your personal manager will most likely be involved in negotiating recording, publishing, merchandising, and production contracts. In conjunction with your booking agent, he will oversee the booking and routing of concert tours and coordinate the sale of merchandise at these performances. He will be also responsible for seeking tour support from your record label. This includes financial support as well as support through marketing, advertising, and local promotions. He will hire a tour manager and, in some cases, a production manager, who will hire the remaining tour staff.

Overseeing every detail of an artist's career is no small feat, and it requires mutual trust between you and your personal manager. As an artist, you should have input regarding important business decisions—but you must empower your manager to do his job. This has real benefits for you. An artist with established personal management has created a buffer between himself and the industry, thus freeing up his time and energy for creative endeavors. After all, creating music is your most important function as an artist.

Early in your career, you may not possess the power to attract the interest of high-caliber management. In fact, your manager may be someone who is relatively unknown. That's okay—being the underdog isn't necessarily a bad thing. What's important is that your manager is competent and enthusiastic, and that he shares your artistic vision. Many times, "unknown" managers go on to build entertainment empires. This isn't to say that signing with an established manager is a bad idea—but the manager's track record shouldn't be your only consideration. Sometimes a new artist gets lost in the shuffle at a large firm, because those firms are more inclined to look after their established acts. Remember that your manager's status may not have as much to do with his effectiveness as his commitment and availability.

When you're considering a manager, it's a good idea to check his credentials. Ask his other clients how they view his work. Take a look at the success they have (or haven't) had with him. Set up a meeting with your potential manager and

THE MANAGER IS A KEY MEMBER OF THE
TEAM. PICTURED HERE ARE THE MEAT
PUPPETS WITH THEN-MANAGER
JACKSON HARING.

his associates to determine if the vibes are good. Don't be afraid to go into this meeting with a list of topics you'd like to discuss. Typical questions would include the length of the contract, his rate of commission, which of his expenses will be charged back to you, and whether he will be acting as your "hands-on" representative. You should most certainly ask him what he feels he can do for both your short- and long-term career. Your manager is going to be a key member of your team and potentially will have a lot of responsibility. He stands to make a lot of money from you, so you'd better feel comfortable with the terms of the management contract he's offering. It's important that you have full confidence in his ability to represent you. Don't be intimidated, and never lose sight of the fact that *you* are the one doing the hiring.

It pays to be clear up front about the tasks you wish your manager to perform, some of which I mentioned earlier. Since the term "personal management" means different things to different people, this may be the time to set up some working parameters. For instance, I personally make it a rule not to call my manager outside of office hours unless it's a dire emergency. I don't ask him or his staff to look after my personal affairs outside of band business. I find these personal requests take time away from the professional matters the manager was hired to handle.

Every artist-management contract is unique. Since the contract will be binding for a time period to be determined through your negotiations, you may wish to stipulate obligations that must be fulfilled in order for the contract to continue. These stipulations could include securing recording, publishing, and merchandising contracts as well as equipment endorsements.

In the music industry, managers usually receive between 10 and 20 percent of the artist's gross earnings—that is, the

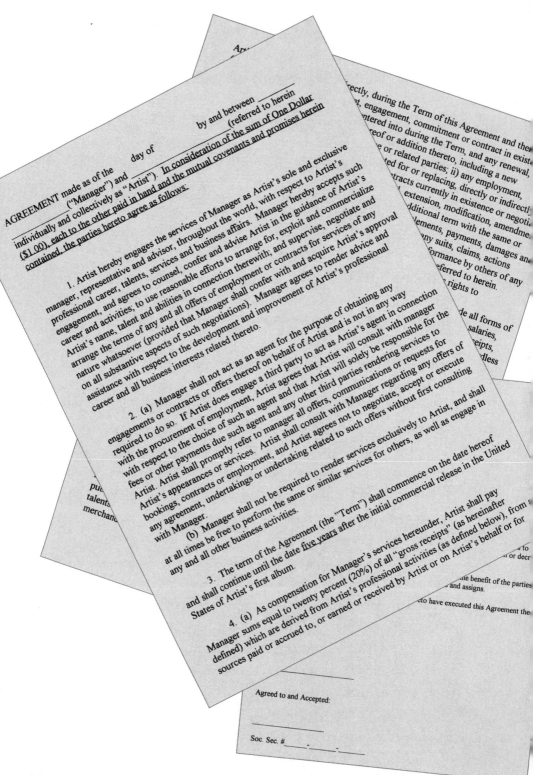

AGREEMENT made as of the _____ day of _____ by and between _____ (referred to herein ("Manager") and _____ (referred to herein individually and collectively as "Artist"). In consideration of the sum of One Dollar ($1.00), each to the other paid in hand and the mutual covenants and promises herein contained, the parties hereto agree as follows:

1. Artist hereby engages the services of Manager as Artist's sole and exclusive manager, representative and advisor, throughout the world, with respect to Artist's professional career, talents, services and business affairs. Manager hereby accepts such engagement, and agrees to counsel, confer and advise Artist in the guidance of Artist's career and activities; to use reasonable efforts to arrange for, exploit and commercialize Artist's name, talent and abilities in connection therewith; and supervise, negotiate and arrange the terms of any and all offers of employment or contracts for services of any nature whatsoever (provided that Manager shall confer with and acquire Artist's approval on all substantive aspects of such negotiations). Manager agrees to render advice and assistance with respect to the development and improvement of Artist's professional career and all business interests related thereto.

2. (a) Manager shall not act as an agent for the purpose of obtaining any engagements or contracts or offers thereof on behalf of Artist and is not in any way required to do so. If Artist does engage a third party to act as Artist's agent in connection with the procurement of employment, Artist agrees that Artist will consult with manager with respect to the choice of such an agent and that Artist will solely be responsible for the fees or other payments due such agent and any other third parties rendering services to Artist. Artist shall promptly refer to manager all offers, communications or requests for Artist's appearances or services. Artist shall consult with Manager regarding any offers of bookings, contracts or employment, and Artist agrees not to negotiate, accept or execute any agreement, undertakings or undertaking related to such offers without first consulting with Manager.

(b) Manager shall not be required to render services exclusively to Artist, and shall at all times be free to perform the same or similar services for others, as well as engage in any and all other business activities.

3. The term of the Agreement (the "Term") shall commence on the date hereof and shall continue until the date five years after the initial commercial release in the United States of Artist's first album.

4. (a) As compensation for Manager's services hereunder, Artist shall pay Manager sums equal to twenty percent (20%) of all "gross receipts" (as hereinafter defined) which are derived from Artist's professional activities (as defined below), from sources paid or accrued to, or earned or received by Artist or on Artist's behalf or for

Agreed to and Accepted:

_____

Soc. Sec. # ____ - ____ - ____

earnings before taxes and expenses are deducted. The exact figure varies from manager to manager. It's standard operating procedure that management *does not* receive commission from recording and video budgets, unless there's money awarded to the artist during the project or upon completion. A word to the wise regarding advances: Since your manager takes his commission up front, be careful not to mortgage your future by taking ridiculously large advances that could require years to recoup. Your manager will have gotten his cut, while you, on the other hand, will be stuck paying back the advance. (There will be more about advances in the "Record Deals & Artist Royalties" section, page 48.)

You may have other considerations that will apply to your management situation. Whatever the terms of the agreement may be, don't forget that this decision is one of the most important ones you will make in advancing your career—so take your time and investigate every aspect carefully.

THERE'S NOTHING WRONG WITH ABSORBING AS MUCH INFORMATION AS POSSIBLE TO HELP ESTABLISH A GAME PLAN.

In Ohio, where we're from, we played three sets a night in the bars. We were pressing our own records, and we'd set up a turntable between sets as a way to pitch them. The first time we went to New York, somebody from a record company approached us and said, "I'd like to put you guys out on my label. Do you have girlfriends with jobs who can support you?" We said, "Well, we think we'll wait for a better offer!"

You never know what will happen. We didn't have any expectations for the song "Whip It." We had another song on the album that we thought was the hit. We were on the road, and halfway through the tour somebody said, "Man, all these discos in Miami are going crazy over 'Whip It.' It's a breakout hit!"

—Bob Mothersbaugh

GUITARIST FOR DEVO

ATTORNEYS

AS ATTRACTIVE AS ANY CONTRACT MAY APPEAR, MOST OF us would be hard pressed to sift through all the legal mumbo-jumbo to see what it really says. That's why we hire attorneys. Lawyers are key players on any musical team, and having an expert legal eagle on your side can be quite beneficial. Without one, contract negotiation and courtroom litigation are virtually impossible.

Modern law is very specialized, so your primary attorney should be one who practices music-business law. Where can you find such a specialist? For the most part, they're located in the major music-business cities: Los Angeles, New York, Nashville, and London. Attorneys are networked throughout the world, though, so don't fret if you live somewhere else. You may already have a relationship with an attorney specializing in another field of law; if so, ask him for a referral to a music-business attorney. There are also directories where you will find listings for such services; these are found in such places as *Performance* magazine, *The Yellow Pages of Rock*, and various *Billboard* publications.

Some artists have difficulty finding personal management when they're starting out, so they opt to have their attorney fill in as their temporary manager. This approach should be avoided if at all possible. Problems can arise if there are going to be any royalties due from whatever deals the attorney secures while acting as your manager. He may even waive his legal fees in exchange for these royalties. This may not seem like a big deal at the time, but when a personal manager finally gets hired, you may find that both your manager and your attorney want a portion of these royalties.

In another scenario, the attorney could act in your behalf by securing recording, publishing, and merchandising deals before your management is in place. This can ultimately take away your leverage in securing the manager you prefer. The attorney may have eaten up all the deal points, leaving no financial incentive for a manager to work with your band. You could find yourself in a situation where you're heavily indebted to your attorney and highly unattractive to qualified personal managers.

These situations generally occur when you have not yet secured personal management and funds are low at the time of inking a deal with an attorney. Think twice before entering into this type of agreement. The best way to avoid this is to hire an attorney based on his legal expertise and flair for negotiation, not his management abilities. In my opinion, an attorney is not a good replacement for a personal manager. Your attorney and your manager are both valuable members of your team—but they should be separate members.

When you hire an attorney, you will have to pay a fee to retain his services. This could be anywhere from several hundred to several thousand dollars, depending on the caliber of the attorney. Aside from retainers, attorneys make their money by billing their clients on an hourly basis. If a major task needs tending to, such as a record-label negotiation, it may be to everyone's advantage to pay your attorney a predetermined fee. (Since this type of negotiation can be long and drawn out, the hourly billing could be very costly.) If it can be avoided, these deals should not include any royalties for the attorney. Another thing to remember is that every time you call or meet with your attorney, the clock starts ticking. You will be billed for these precious moments—so be precise and get right to the point.

The best way for you to keep a proper perspective on the people who work for you is to let them work in the areas where they are experts. You will need an attorney in your corner at all times, looking out for your best interests—so find the best one you can and make sure he tends to your legal business, not your management concerns. This will allow you to concentrate on music while he handles the tedious details of the law.

AN ATTORNEY PLAYS A VERY IMPORTANT ROLE IN AN ARTIST'S CAREER—HIRE ONE BASED ON HIS LEGAL EXPERTISE AND FLAIR FOR NEGOTIATION.

BOOKING AGENCIES

PERFORMING ARTISTS RELY ON BOOKING AGENCIES TO secure, schedule, and route live gigs for them. Early in my career, I spent a great deal of time trying to drum up interest from the local agencies in different parts of Minnesota. I had figured out that this was the ticket to getting good gigs. In fact, it can be almost impossible to book decent shows without an agency acting as a middleman between you and the promoter or club owner. Securing the attention of an agency usually involves inviting them to a show or even putting together some sort of showcase to prove your worth as a live act.

To work with a booking agency, you will need to put together a promotional kit the agent can send out to potential gig situations. These kits usually include a black-and-white 8"x10" photo of the group, a biography, a current set list (when I was starting out, most aspiring bands in the Midwest had to have cover songs in their repertoire, especially to play dances, bars, and clubs), and posters the promoter can use as advertisements for the upcoming show. (Our posters had a photo, the name of the group, and a blank spot at the bottom where the date, time, and location of the show could be handwritten.)

When an artist signs a deal with a large agency, he will usually have one particular agent responsible for looking after his affairs. This agent is commonly referred to as the "responsible agent" or RA. Working under the RA's direction, the other agents of the company book performances within their geographical territories. Some artists sign with one agency to book their domestic performances and a different one to handle foreign countries. Some agencies book their artists exclusively worldwide.

DAVE MUSTAINE

NICK MENZA

DAVID ELLEFSON

MARTY FRIEDMAN

MEGADETH

Photo: Gene Kirkland / 1992

TO WORK WITH A BOOKING AGENCY, YOU WILL NEED TO PUT TOGETHER A PROMOTIONAL KIT THE AGENT CAN SEND OUT.

THIS CONTRACT for the personal services of musicians/artist on the engagement described herein, made between the undersigned Purchaser of Music (herein called "EMPLOYER") and the undersigned leader represents musicians/artists.

The musicians/artists are engaged severally on the terms and conditions on the face of this contract. The undersigned leader represents and guarantees that the musicians/artists designated herein have agreed to be bound by the terms and conditions hereof. Each musician/artist to be designated at a later time, upon acceptance, shall be bound by the terms and conditions under the undersigned leader.

1. Engagement (Location) _____ Hall Manager: _____
    (Address) _____

2. Band or Group Name _____
3. SOUND CHECK MANDATORY. _____ TIX: _____
4. NO TAX DEDUCTIONS ALLOWABLE. _____ /Capacity: _____
5. Engagement date (s) _____

6. Type of Engagement _____ GROSS POTENTIAL _____

7. WAGE AGREED UPON _____

8. The wages disclosed herein include all expenses Employer has agreed to reimburse in accordance with the attached schedule, or a schedule to be provided Employer on or before date of engagement.
9. It is expressly understood by all parties hereto that the Employer has no right to control the manner, means, and details of the performance of services by the musicians/artists including the leader as well as the ends to be accomplished. On behalf of Employer the leader will on the engagement and Employer has no right to supervise the services of the musicians/artists subject to proven detention by personal illness, accidents,
10. The obligation of musicians /artists to performance services hereunder is subject to proven detention by personal illness, accidents, riots, strikes, acts of God, or other legitimate conditions beyond musicians/artists control. On behalf of Employer the leader will distribute monies received from Employer to musicians, including himself, as specified below, or as specified on a separate memorandum provided to Employer at or before commencement of the employment hereunder and take and turn over to Employer receipts therefore from each musician/artist, including himself. The amount of money paid to the leader includes the cost of transportation, which will be reported by the Employer and the musician(s) who ar parties to this contract that neither International Creative
11. It is expressly understood by the Employer and the musician(s) who ar parties to this contract in any capacity and that neither International Creative Management, Inc. nor its officers are parties to this contract in any capacity and that neither International Creative Management, Inc. nor its officers are liable for the performance breach of any provisions hereof.
12. Employer and Artist agree that receipt of this contract and commencement of performance shall be adequate confirmation of all terms embodied in this contract and rider, and shall be binding on all parties, whether the contract is signed or not.

X _____

X _____

An agent's job can become a game of trading favors with concert promoters, especially when he's trying to break a new artist. I'll give you a hypothetical example: An agency signs a new artist who has little road experience or guarantee of ticket sales. The agency also has artists who are established and continually sell large numbers of concert tickets in most of the markets they play. So the agency calls upon a promoter, one who has booked their more established artists, and asks him to take a risk on booking a show or series of shows for their new artist. Out of good faith, the promoter agrees to book the show(s), even if it means losing money the first time out. The promoter is betting on the new artist's potential, hoping that his career will blossom and make him a profit in future performances. He also knows he has a better shot at getting the agency to continue delivering their established artists to him in the future if he does this. As they say in showbiz, "One hand washes the other."

Some agencies handle a variety of artists in different fields, such as musicians, actors, comedians, writers, film directors, etc. Other agencies operate on a smaller scale and may specialize in booking strictly musical talent. Whatever the case may be, productivity and leverage are the real concerns when hiring an agency. Productivity is easy to gauge—either the agency gets you work or it doesn't. By leverage, I mean the power an agency has in packaging tours. For example, if you sign with an agency that has many other artists in the same genre of music you play, you will stand a better chance for successful tour packaging. (Of course, if they have too many similar acts, you could get overlooked.)

It's standard procedure for an agency to collect 10 to 15 percent of the income from an artist's performances for the engagements they have booked. Like the management fee, this is taken from gross income—so with an agency and management both receiving commissions from your performances, you could be paying out as much as 35 percent of your income before expenses. This has a major effect on your ability to stay on the road—more about this later.

PERFORMING ARTISTS RELY ON BOOKING AGENCIES. PRODUCTIVITY AND LEVERAGE ARE THE PRIMARY CONCERNS.

BUSINESS MANAGEMENT

AS YOUR CAREER STARTS TO TAKE OFF, MONEY WILL BEGIN to change hands quickly. At this point, it's appropriate to hire a business manager. Business management differs from personal management in that the business manager's primary job is handling the financial end of your career. This includes, but is not limited to, the collection of funds from royalty sources, tours, and merchandising.

A business manager oversees his client's finances, and his staff of bookkeepers will handle the routine financial chores of paying bills, doing payroll, setting up insurance policies, and—most important—handling tax matters. Some firms offer their clients investment suggestions as well—but, in my opinion, the best business managers refer their clients to outside firms that specialize in investments. Good business managers would like to see their clients hang onto their hard-earned money rather than get involved in risky investment schemes.

Business management firms are either paid on an hourly basis or receive a percentage of the artist's gross earnings. In most cases, they receive a percentage of the gross; five percent is the industry standard, but keep in mind that there are exceptions to the rule.

If you were to average a successful artist's earnings, substantial as they may seem, over the entire span of his career, the numbers might not be so impressive. In some cases, they could be only slightly better than minimum wage! So when a business manager advises you to save your money, it's wise to listen to him. Let's face it—we earn our money in an unstable way, so it's wise to use stable investment strategies. Never lose sight of the fact that the sun will eventually set on your career. It's essential to have money stashed away, or you could have nothing to show for all of your hard work.

We've all heard the horror stories about famous people who have squandered their fortunes with bad investing or extravagant lifestyles. My early business-management experiences were rather unpleasant, due to my youth and financial ignorance. I was grateful when my all-too-frequent requests for cash were finally, albeit reluctantly, honored. I soon discovered that because my spending habits were out of control, my accountant was not able to withhold the necessary state and federal taxes. As a result, I found myself buried very deep in "tax hell" and spent the next few years digging my way out. All was not lost, though—I had learned a valuable lesson, one that certainly influenced the way I manage my money today. Never forget that your business managers may advise you on how to handle money matters, but ultimately the financial responsibility lies with the client: *you*.

New York bassist Will Lee (who plays in the band on *Late Show with David Letterman* as well as doing loads of session work) shared with me this account of one of his financial experiences—one where complacency on his part cost him a lot of money: "I gave my accounting firm total control over my finances, and an employee within that organization managed to split with $45,000 of my money in a year and a half. Even though I could blame the accountants themselves—after all, I had hired them so foolish things wouldn't happen with my money—there's a lesson to be learned. You have to be really on top of these things." The point here is not to instill fear in you about accounting firms, but simply to show that assuming other people will automatically handle everything for you could leave you financially high and dry if you're not careful.

One way to combat these problems is to set up a method of approval for withdrawing funds and paying bills. This will protect both you and your bookkeeper from sticky misunderstandings. Nothing is worse than a lack of communication, especially when money is involved, so being thorough is to everyone's advantage. At the end of the day, we're all ultimately responsible for our own financial affairs.

IT'S A GOOD IDEA TO HAVE A BUSINESS MANAGER TO HANDLE MONEY MATTERS. BUT ULTIMATELY THE FINANCIAL RESPONSIBILITY LIES WITH THE CLIENT: YOU.

Photo by Ebet Roberts

Music is not only my career, it's my main hobby. My advice has always been: "Don't do it for the money." When I first came to New York, I was hired by a band called Dreams, and that was the most amazing stroke of luck you could imagine! The guitar player in that band also helped me to get studio gigs playing and singing on jingles.

In 1975 Paul Shaffer produced the band I was in, the 24th Street Band. Around that time, he got a call to do music for a late-night pilot, and he asked me if I wanted to do it. I said, "Sure. When do we start?" He said, "Next week." So we learned some tunes—and the show took off.

—Will Lee

BASSIST FOR *THE LATE SHOW WITH DAVID LETTERMAN*

PART
THREE

RECORDING

GETTING TO KNOW YOUR RECORD LABEL

BEHIND THE ROWS OF GOLD AND PLATINUM RECORDS that line the walls of most record-company offices is a complex network of people working together to sell records. Even before you secure a record deal, it's a good idea to learn how a record company operates—and once you've been signed, it's essential. Understanding how your label operates is very important to your career, and it's in your best interest to familiarize yourself with the people who put in so many hours selling your music.

It takes a large staff to effectively carry out the vast assortment of tasks handled by a record company. To help you get a better idea of how it all works, the following is a brief walk-through (in alphabetical order) of the various major departments within a typical record company:

A&R (Artists and Repertoire). These are the talent scouts for the label. Their job consists of finding talent and then working with the artists on a creative level. This includes song and producer selection as well as finding outside songwriters, when needed.

Accounting/Finance. These folks handle finances for the label, which includes the computing and distributing of artists' royalties.

Artist Development. This department is responsible for

Photo by Ebet Roberts

JOURNEY SHOWS OFF A COUPLE OF THEIR GOLD ALBUMS.

"working" the artists' records, especially when they're touring. They coordinate such things as radio and television promotions and tour support. They also see that the local vendors stock the company's records on their shelves.

Business Affairs. They negotiate contracts and set up licensing deals for the label's artists. Business affairs also approves requests made by artist-development personnel for tour support as well as overseeing budgets for such things as promotion and video. The staff may include attorneys, accountants, and business experts.

International. This department oversees and coordinates the label's duties regarding an album's release, promotion, press, and sales in foreign countries.

Marketing. In conjunction with the promotion and publicity departments, marketing develops strategies for advertising and selling the label's product. They're also concerned with making sure records are available for vendors to sell.

Product Management. This department is the engine that drives the machine. They're in charge of coordinating all the various departments to work *together.* At some labels, these responsibilities are divided amongst the various departments but handled mainly by A&R.

Production. They make the arrangements and oversee the manufacturing of records, tapes, and CDs as well as shipping them to distributors and outlets.

Promotion. This department works in conjunction with marketing but sticks primarily to getting radio airplay for new releases. They are the all-time schmoozers. God bless them!

JELLYFISH CELEBRATES AT A
PROMOTIONAL PARTY WITH
THEIR RECORD COMPANY STAFF.

Publicity/Press. The people who work in this department are responsible for the artists' exposure in the media. They arrange press conferences, interviews (print, radio, and television), and photo sessions as well as handling other press-related events and activities.

Sales. In conjunction with marketing, sales is responsible for making product available to stores and outlets. They also monitor the sales of product and report to the other departments as well as artist management.

Video. As the name indicates, this department coordinates and oversees all aspects of video production and promotion. They are responsible for jamming the music-video networks to get airplay.

These brief descriptions cover the major departments you may encounter, but it's important to remember that no two labels operate in exactly the same fashion. For instance, some of these departments may have a hierarchy of executives to whom they must report, i.e., president, vice president, manager, etc.

At the end of the day, it's no fluke when a record achieves massive success. It takes a lot of hard work and effort to orchestrate all these forces—and when this is done well, the rewards can be very sweet for everyone involved.

UNDERSTANDING HOW YOUR LABEL OPERATES IS VERY IMPORTANT. AND IT'S IN YOUR BEST INTEREST TO FAMILIARIZE YOURSELF WITH IT.

RECORD DEALS & ARTIST ROYALTIES

ARTISTS CREATE A COMMODITY, WHICH IS MUSIC; RECORD LABELS market and sell this commodity. This is a vital relationship. Signing a deal with a competent label and having a good working relationship with the company is of the utmost importance for your success and career longevity.

These days, most major record labels seem to be taking a short-term approach to artists' careers rather than viewing them as long-term projects. This means you may not have a multiple-album chance to establish yourself—so you'd better hope that your debut is a success. I feel this is due, at least in part, to the rapid changes in the music industry brought on by the video age. You have only a quick shot at establishing your recording career, so you'd better have your act together and be very clear about your musical vision *before* you sign a major-label recording deal.

It helps to have an "in" (contact) at the label who will listen to your music. If you don't have one, you should send your demo to the attention of the A&R department. In my experience, the demo should consist of no more than three of your best tracks with absolutely no filler material, extended intros, or musically self-indulgent songs. A&R people hear a lot of music, and they aren't likely to give you a second thought if your music is anything less than captivating and to the point.

Due to the affordability of good home-studio equipment,

this is the age of do-it-yourself recording and manufacturing of CD demos. While it can be helpful to sell your CD directly to the public, this type of package is not nearly as impressive as you might think to a major-label A&R person. After all, if you've gone this far to package your music, what's left for them to do? At this stage of your career, don't let the delusion that you need a "complete package" stand in the way of inventive songwriting and charisma. It's the music that counts!

Aside from making, distributing, and promoting recordings, labels loan you money interest-free so you can make records, film videos, and promote tours. One big myth that many young musicians have been led to believe is that the record company will pay for everything. Not so. While a label will advance money to artists in order to cover their costs, you must remember that an advance is nothing more than a loan that will have to be paid back to the record company out of your royalty earnings. This is known as the advance/recoupment process, and it's how the recording industry works.

The label will collect their money *before* any royalties are paid to you. This is why it takes some recording artists several years to maneuver themselves into a situation where they can actually make any real money from record sales. Yes, you can become famous playing music and still not see a penny—unless you keep a close eye on those advances!

Some artists choose not to use the label for funding their recordings. In these cases, the artists pay for their own recording sessions. By doing this, they can deliver a master recording to the label for a cash advance against future sales. Or they may choose not to take an advance at all, thus avoiding the advance/recoupment process completely. Of course, this requires a large sum of money up front, which is why it

DUE TO THE AFFORDABILITY OF GOOD HOME-STUDIO
EQUIPMENT, THIS IS THE AGE OF DO-IT-YOURSELF
RECORDING. PICTURED HERE: PRIMUS HARD AT WORK
IN THEIR HOME-RECORDING STUDIO.

isn't very common. But for those who have the option, it can be the ideal way to go.

Let's take a look at a hypothetical deal in which a band receives an advance to make a record. After the recording is completed, the label advances more money to shoot a video and to cover expenses for a tour. As you can see, the debt adds up quickly:

Recording budget	$150,000.00
Producer's fee	30,000.00
Video	100,000.00
Tour support	20,000.00
Total	$300,000.00

Now let's see how the advance gets recouped by the label. The money the band earns for each copy of the record sold is their *artist royalty*. This royalty is based on the suggested retail price of the recording; for this example, let's use a cassette as the recording medium. These days, artist royalties are roughly 10 to 20 percent of the list price (often referred to as 10 to 20 "points"). To determine the actual royalty, you must first subtract 20 percent for packaging costs (slightly less for vinyl and more for compact discs).

Retail price of cassette	$9.98
20% packaging cost	-1.98
Royalty base	$8.00

At a royalty rate of 10 percent, this amounts to $.80 per copy sold. At this rate, the royalty for selling 100 cassettes would be $80. But wait—for promotional reasons, the label has allotted 15 percent for complimentary (free) goods. The band does not receive royalties on free goods, which means they actually get paid for only 85 records rather than 100. This translates to $68 for 100 copies *sold*, or $.68 per copy.

Royalty computations reflect records sold, not records shipped. Regardless of how many records get shipped to the stores, the label pays the artist only for the ones that are actually sold by retailers. Okay, the band owes $300,000 in advance money—so, in this scenario, they would have to sell more than 400,000 units to break even with the label (441,177 X $.68 = $300,000). From that point on, provided there were no more advances, the band would turn a profit from their record sales.

There's another way you can handle this: Fund your own record production and license the master tapes to a record distributor, thus netting a higher royalty rate. Although distribution deals have this advantage, they usually mean limited advertising and promotion only in restricted territories— which often translates to lower sales. If you sign a full record deal with a label, you will receive the benefit of the label's in-house promotion and publicity departments. In addition, most major labels distribute and promote records worldwide.

Record sales are measured by various standards around the world. In the U.S., sales are calculated by a system called Soundscan, which is the official sales report to *Billboard* magazine. Soundscan tracks the sale of each record as it is scanned at the counters of retail stores. Not all stores have Soundscan, however, so the weekly charts that reflect nationwide sales are not completely accurate. For this reason, total sales may be slightly more than indicated by the charts.

Record labels send their artists royalty statements at regular intervals, usually quarterly or semi-annually. Due to varying accounting and reporting methods outside the U.S., there is often a delay in obtaining accurate sales figures. Royalty statements reflect the number of records sold and the dollar amount earned within a stated period. You may receive statements reflecting sales that took place six months to a year previously. This can be alarming at first, but it's the way some labels work.

For most professional musicians, a record deal is the backbone of a strong career. You should know how these deals work, and I hope this chapter has given you a start in understanding the way the royalty system operates. At the very least, you should know how difficult it can be to pay back a large advance! Remember to keep your advances and your overhead low, so the accrued debt does not wipe out your profits.

RECORD LABELS ARE IN THE BUSINESS OF SELLING MUSIC. HAVING A GOOD WORKING RELATIONSHIP WITH A LABEL IS OF THE UTMOST IMPORTANCE TO YOUR SUCCESS AND CAREER LONGEVITY.

INDEPENDENT RECORD LABELS

INDEPENDENT RECORD LABELS HAVE BECOME QUITE popular lately. Indies offer many artists their only shot at a recording career, especially ones who don't have large commercial appeal or those who are looking for more artistic freedom than they can get with a big record company. An independent label can also be just the ticket for artists who have a loyal following but can't quite seem to clinch a major-label deal. Often times these artists are poised for success, and an indie release with substantial sales can be just what they need to attract the attention of a major label.

Mike Varney has given numerous musicians a shot at a recording career through his independent label, Shrapnel Records. In Mike's opinion, "Major labels can be a sink-or-swim situation for an artist. Independent labels, on the other hand, have a greater ability to stick with artists for a longer period of time—to let them develop, to give them encouragement, and to provide them with the tools to grow." Once again, this drives home the point that we currently live in a fast-paced musical situation in which many of today's newer major-label artists do not have the luxury of multiple album releases to develop their careers.

Generally, the royalty rates offered by independent labels are similar to those of major labels, but artists often receive considerably smaller advances—perhaps as little as $5,000 to

Photo by Ebet Roberts

SOME INDIES SIGN DEALS WITH MAJOR LABELS FOR DISTRIBUTION. THIS MEANS THAT AN INDIE ARTIST'S RECORD WILL BE PLACED IN THE SAME STORES WHERE THE MAJORS PLACE THEIR PRODUCTS.

$10,000—and they may not get the radio and video promotion they would get with a major. Indies usually will not advance money for tour support, and they may have a much smaller and more specialized A&R department. This means that preparation for recording is of the utmost importance, and the strategic use of other sources of income (such as touring and merchandise) may be vital to career survival for the indie artist.

This does not mean that an artist signed to an independent label won't make money from record sales. Keep in mind that indie labels usually look to sell somewhere in the neighborhood of 10,000 to 50,000 records for their artists. If you use the royalty calculations from the previous chapter, you'll see that with a smaller advance the artist stands to recoup and start making a profit sooner, even though overall sales may be much lower. And, because independent labels don't have as much overhead as major labels do, they stand to make money much more quickly, too. This is one big reason why some indies have been able to survive the changing musical trends over the years.

Some indies sign deals with major labels for distribution. This means that even though an artist is signed to an independent label, his record will be placed in the same stores where the majors place their products. This can be the best of both worlds for the artist, giving him more freedom to record while assuring that his records will be distributed on a much larger scale than if they were distributed exclusively by an independent.

As I mentioned earlier, a deal with an indie can be a fantastic steppingstone to a major-label contract. Keep in mind that the indies are aware of this, and they sometimes stand to reap great financial rewards if this comes to pass. This is accomplished either by a buyout from the major

INDEPENDENT LABELS, SUCH AS THESE SHOWCASED AT AN INDIE TRADESHOW, OFFER MANY MUSICIANS THE ARTISTIC FREEDOM THAT THEY CAN'T GET WITH A BIG RECORD COMPANY.

(where the big record company pays cash for the artist's contract) or through an override from the royalties earned by the new label's contract. In all fairness, the indie label is certainly entitled to some compensation, since they took the initial risk on the artist—but as an artist, this is an important issue for you to be aware of, since it may affect the point structure of your new major-label deal.

Independent labels can provide services and opportunities that may not be available elsewhere. Since indies are very "street oriented" in their approach to music (and many specialize in specific musical styles), up-and-coming artists stand a good chance of actually getting their demo tapes heard by indie A&R people. So if you're shopping for a label, you may wish to approach an independent label that specializes in your type of music. Keep in mind, however, that when you're pursuing *any* recording deal—indie or major—strong musical material, hard work, and perseverance are proven factors in securing a long-term career.

INDEPENDENT LABELS OFFER MANY ARTISTS THEIR ONLY SHOT AT A RECORDING CAREER, AND A DEAL WITH AN INDIE CAN BE A STEPPINGSTONE TO A MAJOR-LABEL CONTRACT.

# MUSIC PUBLISHING

IN ADDITION TO THE ARTIST ROYALTY, THERE IS ANOTHER type of royalty you need to know about: the *mechanical* royalty. This is the fee paid to a songwriter by a label for the right to use his song on a recording. This brings us to the important subject of music publishing. A music publisher is a business that collects mechanical royalties from record labels and pays them to songwriters for a percentage of the money. Here are four good reasons why you should consider working with a music publisher:

1. They offer their writers a cash advance.
2. They will shop songs to other recording artists looking for material.
3. They try to place songs in films, commercials, and television shows.
4. They handle the collection and administration of royalties.

Pianist/singer/songwriter Tori Amos educated herself on music publishing by making friends with publishers; she then decided how she wanted to handle the publishing for her own material. "I own my own publishing," she explains, "meaning that I don't have a deal with an outside publisher. I hired my parents to collect the money for me. I generate the most income with the songs I write, and this way I know where that money is. People want copyrights more than anything in this business—everybody wants your songs, and they want to pay as little as possible for them. I don't necessarily recommend this approach to most people, though—what's right for me may not be right for someone else." Amos points out that controlling her own publishing is not just about money but also about freedom. "The one thing that I do have control over is my songs. Nobody can tell me what to do with them. I feel really inspired to write, because nobody can control my songs."

While this approach works well for Tori Amos, most songwriters enter into agreements with music-publishing firms. There are many types of publishing deals, but for our purposes we'll consider three. The first is the *exclusive songwriter* deal, where as a songwriter you basically work for the music publisher; even though you are paid royalties for your songs, the publisher owns the rights to them. Second is the *co-publishing* deal, where the writer generally splits all income 50-50 with the publisher. (The publisher's portion is called the publisher's share, and the writer's portion is called the writer's share.) The third type is the *standard administration* deal, where the songwriter retains complete ownership of his songs and pays the publisher 10 percent for doing the administrative work.

Another benefit of having a music publisher is that the publisher will secure copyrights for your songs. Even though there is a financial sacrifice on your part, as the songwriter, it's usually well worth it to let the publisher handle the business, so you can spend more time creating. It's also difficult for an artist to try to do everything himself—remember, 100 percent of nothing is nothing!

If you don't need a cash advance or you don't have any interest in your songs being recorded by anyone else, you may decide against using a music publisher. This will, however, limit your opportunities for growth and income. There are many songwriters who don't have a recording deal of their own but write songs strictly so their music publisher can pitch them to recording artists. We hear many songs on the radio each day that are written and recorded in this fashion, even though we tend to associate a song with the artist who performs it.

In a band, the songwriting contributions may vary greatly—and the way in which the writing credit, and therefore the publishing money, is divided can become an area of concern. The splits can be done in many ways, and I recommend negotiating this point early on with the other band members to eliminate any misunderstandings. Everyone should be clear about what they will be receiving *before* any advances are taken.

I'd like to show you how publishing royalties work, and for the sake of simplicity we'll talk about a full-length album. Royalties are paid on what's known as the statutory rate, which is currently 6.95 cents per composition. (This rate is always changing.) On an album, you will generally be paid for a maximum of ten songs—which means that if you put 13 songs on the album, you'll be paid only for ten of them. In the U.S., you will be paid 75 percent of this 6.95 cents, which works out to 5.21 cents per song. In most cases, this 75 percent rate also applies in Canada; the rate is usually higher elsewhere. Here is the financial breakdown for a co-publishing deal where the writer and publisher split the income evenly:

Statutory rate	$.0695
US & Canada rate @ 75%	$.0521
$.0521 X 10 songs on album	$.521
$.521 X 100,000 records sold	$52,100
Publisher's share (50%)	$26,050
Artist's share (50%)	$26,050

Now, let's say you make a record with five original songs and five cover songs from your favorite classic rock band. The royalty for the cover songs will be paid to the songwriters at the full statutory rate, while your originals will be paid to you at the 75 percent rate, as previously explained. For each record sold, the royalties will be:

Five cover songs at full rate (5 X .0695)	$.35
Five originals at reduced rate (5 X .0695 X .75)	$.26

The mechanical royalty for your originals, assuming 100,000 records are sold, would be $26,000, and the artist's share would be $13,000. You can see why it pays to write your own material!

Another important aspect of music publishing is the service provided by performing-rights societies. The two best-known organizations of this type are BMI (Broadcast Music Incorporated) and ASCAP (American Society of Composers, Authors, and Publishers). These organizations collect a fee whenever one of their songs is played at a nightclub or concert or broadcast by a radio or television station. The money they collect is used to pay the operating expenses of the society, and any remaining portion is divided amongst the participants (songwriters) who belong to the society.

To monitor radio airplay, these societies require stations to keep a log sheet of songs from their daily playlists. For tele-vision, they require the networks to keep cue sheets that list every musical composition played during their programming. The cue sheet also lists how long, how many times, and in what fashion the musical composition is used.

Mechanical royalties can pay big dividends to you as a songwriter, especially if your songs are hits. As we've seen, artist royalties can get eaten up by recoupments of advances for tour support, video, and recording fees—but mechanical royalties don't require any "paybacks" to the record company. (Of course, if you get an advance from the music publisher, this will have to be recouped.) Hit songwriters continue to make a good living from their royalties for many years if their material continues to sell and/or has high radio play. Think about that the next time you listen to a "classic rock" or "oldies" station—the songwriters who wrote those songs are probably still collecting royalties through their music publishers.

MUSIC PUBLISHERS OFFER AN IMPORTANT SERVICE THAT CAN HELP TO MAXIMIZE YOUR INCOME AS A SONGWRITER.

The music business is a cutthroat business, and people are very serious about getting a return on their money. You do yourself a disservice if you don't respect the fact that it is a business, because then you have all these illusions about people being your "friends." They are your friends sometimes, but most of the time it's about business—and if you're not generating money for them, then you're going to be out!

I truly believe you have more freedom if you understand the way the business works. I want my freedom, and I don't want to be a victim. I've heard too many musicians say, "Well, I don't want to get involved in the business end because I don't believe in it." If that's your attitude, then maybe you should just go play in your living room. I don't find the concept of an ignorant musician interesting at all. If you stay ignorant about how the business works, then you will become victimized and blame everyone else.

—Tori Amos

PIANIST/SINGER/SONGWRITER

ADIO PROMOTION

RADIO HAS ALWAYS BEEN AN EFFECTIVE MEANS OF MUSIC promotion. Unfortunately, unless you have a record deal it's extremely difficult to get your songs played on the radio. The exceptions are shows geared toward showcasing local unsigned talent or ones on college stations, which generally have a more liberal programming structure. For the major record companies, contemporary radio is an important tool for promoting artists and boosting record sales. The people responsible for getting songs on the radio are usually part of the label's promotion department. In some cases, independent promotion companies are hired by the label to work specific singles.

The process starts when the record label chooses a single, which is then serviced to designated radio stations via the promotion department. At this point, each station's programming director (PD) will be asked to add the track to the playlist. The promotion staff calls the stations each week to check on the amount of airplay the song is getting. Whenever possible, they will attempt to convince the PD to increase the number of plays the single is getting.

The success of the single may be helped by requests from the station's listeners. The ball is generally set into motion by the label's promo staff, however, so it's important to have enthusiastic go-getters working your record. This is one big

PETE TOWNSHEND
PROMOTES A NEW SONG AT
A SAN FRANCISCO RADIO
STATION IN 1993.

reason why certain songs get an enormous amount of airplay while others don't—it has everything to do with how well the promo people are schmoozing with the programming directors!

There are several different types of radio stations, playing everything from oldies to the latest rock songs, and their playlist activity is measured by Broadcast Data Systems (BDS) and Album Network. These services reflect the week's activities and give the industry an inside tip on current "adds" (additions to the playlist) and "rotations" (number of times played) for records.

While it may appear radio has taken a back seat to music videos, don't underestimate the value of getting your songs played on the radio. In many ways, radio feeds video, which in turn fuels touring and album sales. This is especially true in local markets where concert promoters rely heavily on the local radio stations to promote their events.

RADIO IS A VERY EFFECTIVE MEANS OF PROMOTION—DON'T UNDERESTIMATE ITS IMPORTANCE.

THE VIDEO AGE

WITH THE EXPLOSIVE GROWTH OF THE MUSIC-VIDEO networks, video production has become a major focus for many artists. Most videos are funded, at least in part, by the record label. A respectable record deal will stipulate that the label be responsible for around 50 percent of a reasonably budgeted video. The remaining portion is advanced by the label to the artist and recouped from the artist royalties.

Generally, the songs chosen to be radio singles become videos. This isn't always the case, but it seems to be the most effective way to treat a song in order to get as much promotional mileage from it as possible.

Selecting a video director is usually a team effort involving the label, artist management, and the artist. Most directors have a compilation demo reel of their work to aid potential clients in the selection process. Video directors are selected on the basis of their creative vision and how well it ties in with the artist's musical vision. Once the contenders have been chosen, it's a good idea to meet with them and determine with whom the best working relationship can be established. The directors will sometimes present a treatment at this time—this is basically a story line for the video as it relates to the song. These meetings are a good place to get a feel for the directors' concepts and discuss plans for the video.

Following the selection of a director and treatment, the video goes into preproduction. This stage includes any storyboard rewrites that are necessary, choosing locations to shoot, renting equipment, and hiring the crew and other personnel for the production. Finally, the actual filming begins. After the footage has been shot, the video goes into postproduction. At this point, editing, special effects, and the synchronization of music and pictures take place. This is one

BONO AND THE EDGE OF U2 FILMED THEIR "RATTLE AND HUM" VIDEO IN SAN FRANCISCO.

WITH THE EXPLOSIVE GROWTH OF
THE MUSIC-VIDEO NETWORKS,
VIDEO PRODUCTION HAS BECOME
A MAJOR FOCUS FOR MANY
ARTISTS.

area where you may have a chance to present some of your creative ideas. But don't fret if they're not accepted—after all, directors don't rewrite your songs, so they may not be too keen on you reworking their videos.

When the video is completed, your label will submit it to the appropriate networks. If they accept it, it will then be put into their programming schedules. Bear in mind that networks don't always accept the videos that are presented. Most major record labels have a video production and promotion staff to oversee the entire process, and gaining network acceptance is one of their major concerns.

As far as the networks are concerned, airtime for your video is strictly promotional. Therefore, you will not be paid for any video airplay. If the video is released in a home-video format and sold in record shops, then a royalty will be earned for its sales.

What does it cost? Anywhere from several thousand dollars up into the millions. For this reason, you can see why it pays to be conservative with a video budget, especially early in your career. Always remember that a video is basically a promotional item used to generate record sales.

VIDEO PRODUCTION CAN BE VERY EXPENSIVE—SO IT'S WISE TO BE CONSERVATIVE WITH THE BUDGET.

PRESS, PUBLICITY, AND PROMOTION

IN THE COMPETITIVE WORLD OF MUSIC, IT'S DIFFICULT TO sell a product without an effective promotional campaign. Again, it's the artist's job to make the music and the label's job to sell it—but your cooperation with promotion is essential to your success. As is true with most businesses, promotion lies at the foundation of major sales.

If you're not yet signed and want to solicit potential labels, agents, and managers, you will need to put together an outstanding promotional package. Val Janes, who owns her own marketing company, Fine Tuning, in London, says a press kit should be "attention getting, making you want to pick it up and look at it." It should include a good-quality black-and-white photo, a well-written biography, and possibly even a tape with your best material. Keep in mind that this kit may be your one and only chance to convince others to work with you.

Regarding record-label promotion, we've already established what the label's promo staff does in the areas of video and radio promotion. Publicity is another major factor in helping the promotional wheels to turn; this includes coverage by the media (radio, press, and television) as well as events such as press conferences. At all levels of the game, media exposure is your lifeline to the public—and as an artist's profile increases, so does his media involvement.

Most artists engage in a variety of promotional activities, such as radio, magazine, newspaper, and television interviews as well as in-person record-store signings when they're on tour. It's to everyone's benefit to take advantage of any promotional activities that will help to further your career while still maintaining your integrity. Often, an independent public-relations firm is hired to maximize an artist's promo-

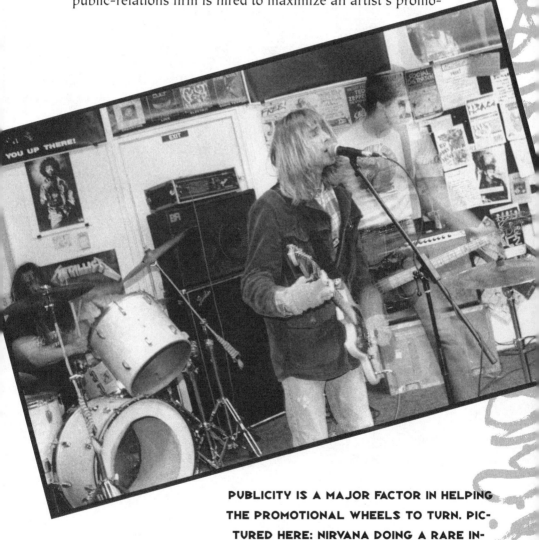

PUBLICITY IS A MAJOR FACTOR IN HELPING THE PROMOTIONAL WHEELS TO TURN. PIC-TURED HERE: NIRVANA DOING A RARE IN-STORE PROMOTIONAL PERFORMANCE AT ROUGH TRADE RECORDS IN 1990.

SLAYER GREETS THEIR FANS IN AN IN-
STORE AUTOGRAPH SIGNING TO
PROMOTE A NEW RECORD.

tional exposure. This firm may be hired by the label or directly by the artist. There are a couple of good reasons for doing this. The first is that the label's publicity demands for all their artists may keep them from being fully effective on your behalf. The second is that if you, the artist, hire the independent publicists, then they will be working for *you*. This can make quite a difference, since most record labels instruct their publicity personnel to work records only while they have "life" (in other words, for a limited period of time) and not necessarily until they have fully run their course. There are many success stories of records that became big sellers only after they had been out for some time—and the promotional cycle had been fully exploited.

Publicist Suzan Crane says her Los Angeles firm is a "conduit between the artist and the media." She also notes that the artist should avoid a "combative relationship" with the record label's publicity department, explaining that the desired goal is to develop a win-win situation involving the artist, the label's publicity department, and an independent publicity firm.

An independent publicist's fee will vary according to the amount of work that needs to be done; it may be paid either by the label or the artist, depending on who did the hiring. In either case, the label should be fully aware that an independent publicist is working the project. Since public-relation firms have one objective—to get their clients noticed by as many people as possible—this can be very helpful in generating media attention.

Your management should work closely with the label's publicity department, and as an artist you should be cooperative. Arranging a press schedule before the release of your record or the beginning of your concert tour is essential. If the budget allows it, a separate promotion/publicity tour can be

PRESS AND PROMOTION LIE AT THE FOUNDATION OF STRONG RECORD SALES.

helpful. It's important to be clear as to how much (if any) of these expenses are recoupable from the artist royalties, because they usually are. For obvious reasons, this should be spelled out by management before the trip.

Most record labels hire a press-clipping service to keep track of their artists' interviews. I've found that reading these clips is useful in evaluating interview style. Stammering, needlessly swearing, or using absent-minded clichés won't make you sound very attractive in print. You should also critique your video and television interviews—repeatedly touching your face, squirming restlessly, or staring off into space can look absolutely ridiculous on film. They, too, can be avoided if you review and evaluate your interviews.

The more adept you become at handling press and publicity, the closer you will come to being a complete professional musician. Overall, I find these supplemental activities very productive and rewarding. You can often see the results in ticket and album sales. Even so, your true success is better measured by how willing you are to work with others and not necessarily by how many records you sell.

PROMOTION THROUGH THE INTERNET

UNLESS YOU'VE BEEN LIVING IN A CAVE, YOU'RE probably aware of—or already involved with—the Internet. While usage of the Net has exploded in the last few years, many people feel it's still in its embryonic stages, and we've only scratched the surface of its real potential. Even so, you can see its growing presence every day, especially since many companies now include their World Wide Web addresses in their advertising campaigns.

Today, it seems if you want to be connected to the rest of the world, you must have an e-mail address. This provides instant delivery and retrieval of messages to people all over the world with the expense of only a local or long-distance telephone call (depending on where you are relative to your provider's access number). This can be extremely helpful for musicians who jump from gig to gig to make their living, as they can stay connected no matter where they are.

If you're in a popular band, e-mail provides a way to stay in touch with your fans. I've used it many times to answer fan mail and respond to requests. Anywhere, anytime, I can simply hook up my laptop computer to read and respond to e-mail messages.

In addition to e-mail, the World Wide Web can be a fantastic way to promote your activities. Again, many artists, including myself, use the Web to stay in touch with their fans.

THE INTERNET IS ALREADY PROVIDING AN INEXPENSIVE WAY TO PROMOTE, ADVERTISE, AND NETWORK THROUGHOUT THE WORLD.

Some artists establish fan clubs in cyberspace as well as design and/or operate their own Web sites. Your Web site can offer a visitor the opportunity to download music as well as photographs, videos, and other graphics. You can also keep your fans abreast of your current activities, because a Web site is usually updated on a regular basis. Some sites offer itineraries of tour dates, set lists, and personal journals as well as chat rooms for fan/artist interaction. However, since there are millions of people trying to draw attention to their products (both musical and non-musical) on the Web, I believe that artists are wise to use the Net in addition to the standard means of promotion: press, radio, and live performance. After all, these methods have been proven successful over the years.

You can either hire a Web-page designer to create your site, or you can do it yourself by learning the necessary codes. When you're ready to go up on a server, you will need to hire an outside company (these are often listed in the business section of local newspapers) for a reasonably low monthly fee, or—if you're technically inclined—you can purchase the necessary computer gear and run it yourself.

Some artists are using the Internet to sell their records directly. I spoke with Andy West about this; Andy is a bassist who used to be in the Dixie Dregs and is now a member of a band called the Mistakes that's using the Web to sell their records. He says, "The Internet is a tremendous asset for groups and individuals who do not have the advantage of a major-label deal, perhaps because they're doing more offbeat or adventuresome music." The Web could be the ultimate form of independent record distribution, since there are no distributors or retail stores to deal with. Of course, the trick is to get paid for the records you sell—depending on your marketing plan, you may wish to sell them C.O.D. as opposed to using the honor system. As more and more artists adopt the do-it-yourself mentality, we're likely see more record distribution via the Web in the future, especially since it offers such massive exposure at a nominal cost.

The Internet is already providing an inexpensive way to promote, advertise, and network throughout the world. Since the entertainment industry likes to hop on the technology bandwagon, it behooves artists at all levels to become computer literate and take advantage of this emerging trend. The long-term effect of Internet marketing remains to be seen, but if it continues to expand at the current rate, it seems the sky's the limit.

THE INTERNET OFFERS EXCITING NEW WAYS TO NETWORK AND DIRECTLY MARKET YOUR MUSIC TO PEOPLE AROUND THE WORLD.

WORKING WITH RECORD PRODUCERS

ONE OF THE KEYS TO MAKING GREAT RECORDS IS THE producer. A good producer should be able to combine songwriting and musical skills of the artist with mode nology to make a timeless recording. He's the one per whose contributions can have the most impact on the and success of a record.

The producer's job is basically to oversee the entir recording process. This includes everything from preparing budgets to utilizing the best available recording techniques in the tracking, overdubbing, mixing, and mastering process. He usually helps to select and arrange songs; in some cases, he may even write songs with the artist.

Many record producers have backgrounds as musicians and/or songwriters. Some are studio engineers who have moved up to the next creative level in their field. Artists with extensive recording experience may wish to produce themselves, assisted by an outstanding studio engineer—but even the most seasoned recording artists often opt to use professional record producers to get the most out of their recordings.

I prefer to view the making of a record as a complete project rather than just a recording session. Getting the producer involved early in the process is a great help in preparing for the actual production work. Most experienced producers and

THE PRODUCER IS THE ONE PERSON WHOSE CONTRIBUTIONS CAN HAVE THE MOST IMPACT ON THE SOUND AND SUCCESS OF A RECORD. PICTURED HERE: JOE SATRIANI AND BAND IN THE RECORDING STUDIO.

recording artists will agree that preproduction is essential—this includes writing, rehearsing, and making demo tapes of the songs *before* going into the studio, where the clock is ticking and the hourly rates are high.

Demo sessions can be done with anything from a 4-track home-recording setup to a fully automated multi-track studio. At this stage, the slickness of the production isn't as important as just getting the material down on tape. There should be some consideration as to how much time and money is invested in preproduction; in a less expensive and more relaxed demo environment, it's often easier to work out the rough spots without feeling pressured. After the demos are made, you can use the tape as a reference to make any necessary alterations before entering the studio. If you haven't selected a producer yet, your demos may be used for shopping potential candidates. Their impressions of your material and suggestions for recording it will help you to evaluate them.

Your A&R rep should be actively involved in selecting a producer. Usually, he can make suggestions based on the track record of the producer and the direction of your music. Producers, much like musicians, have their own unique styles, and you should always consider how a producer's style is going to blend with—or change—your sound.

The producer is usually paid out of the artist royalties. It's up to the artist and the producer to negotiate how many points he will receive for his services. Top-shelf producers often get four to five points per project, and they may even get a portion of the music publishing if they've contributed to the songwriting. Unlike the artist, whose royalties must wait for the recoupment of the recording budget, the producer begins collecting his money as soon as the first record is sold. (If the producer has received an advance, however, it will be recouped against his royalties.)

The producer's point structure often operates on a sliding scale. (This can also apply to the artist royalty.) For instance, the producer may earn four points on the first one million copies sold; after this sales mark is achieved, his payments may increase by another point for the next million sold, and so on. Obviously, this is an incentive plan to encourage both the artist and the producer to contribute their best possible efforts.

THE ALBUM-AND-TOUR CYCLE

SO FAR, WE'VE LOOKED AT MANY OF THE KEY PEOPLE and procedures involved in the making and release of a record. Let's pull all of that together by taking an overview of the process of making a record and then supporting it with a concert tour.

The process starts with songwriting, followed by rehearsal and preproduction (which may include the making of demos). Next you go into the studio for recording, mixing, and mastering. Mastering is almost always done by a professional mastering engineer. (It's his job to take the tape and try to make the final mix sound as uniform as possible with a variety of signal-processing gear—and great ears.) The recording process could take up to a year, although you'd better be a superstar if you want to take that much time! During the recording process, work should be underway on the album-cover artwork and inner-sleeve credits.

When recording is completed, the producer will deliver the mastered product to the record company, whose manufacturing plants will begin production and packaging of cassettes, CDs, and (maybe) LPs. By now, a single will have been chosen; it will be manufactured and shipped to the appropriate radio stations.

A video is usually filmed at this time, and it will be serviced to the video networks. The label also sends advance cassettes (containing the album's music in its entirety, minus the cover artwork) to critics for reviews. Due to the three-month lead time required by most magazines, the press department must schedule interviews and photo shoots to coincide with the release date. The label will ship records to retailers about a week prior to the actual release date. Stores are not permitted to sell product earlier than the scheduled release date.

TOURING GOES HAND IN HAND
WITH THE RELEASE OF A RECORD.
HERE, THE BLACK CROWES
PREPARE TO TAKE TO THE ROAD.

DEPENDING ON THE SUCCESS OF THE RECORD AND THE TOURING DEMAND, THE TOUR CYCLE CAN TAKE YEARS TO COMPLETE. PICTURED HERE: DAVID ELLEFSON ON ONE OF MEGADETH'S NUMEROUS TOURS.

Touring goes hand in hand with the release of a record. The length of a tour is determined by the "buzz" created by the album—the stronger the response, the longer the tour. Touring is simply a means of promoting and selling records as well as such merchandise as T-shirts and other souvenirs. Depending on the success of the record and the touring demand, this cycle can take up to several years to complete.

Anyone who's been through this process knows the album-and-tour cycle can be a real killer. Pacing yourself is crucial to maintaining your sanity, health, and general well-being. It's wise to set aside certain periods of time in order to regroup and keep a healthy perspective. This means there should be appropriately scheduled breaks within the cycle, and this requires intelligent planning on the part of your management. With any luck, you'll get through the cycle in one piece and have a nice chunk of money from successful album sales—and then it will begin all over again.

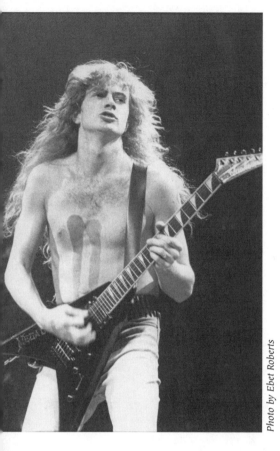

Photo by Ebet Roberts

It can take up to six months to get a record out on the street—and by that time, musical tastes may have changed. You're always playing catch-up, and you're either on the mark or you're out of luck. Trying to copy someone else is not only unoriginal but very risky. Being original and not following trends creates consistency, which is another word for trust. People who listen to me know they can trust me to put out good, consistent music.

—Dave Mustaine

LEAD SINGER/GUITARIST FOR MEGADETH

PART
FOUR

TRAVELING

THE ROAD

PLAYING GOOD LIVE SHOWS IS THE BEST WAY TO ATTRACT the attention of agents, managers, and label A&R personnel. It may also be the only way to pay the bills, especially early in your career when you're desperately trying to become a full-time musician. Seasoned road veteran Joey Ramone, lead singer of the Ramones, says, "The road is where you grow and get tight, and touring is a major part of getting it all together. For us, the road was our bread and butter. We would tour almost all year long and never really stop. That's what it's all about: the live show."

Also, as I explained in the last chapter, touring is the best way to promote a record. If you're a new artist who has just signed a recording contract, your willingness to tour could be a major factor in determining how far the label will go to help you succeed. Slash, guitarist for Guns N' Roses, shares this about the band's early road experiences: "We were signed for a year before we even went into the studio. Then, after we recorded *Appetite for Destruction*, we toured for a year before the record broke. We toured real hard and won over a lot of fans, because we kicked ass and there was a genuine spirit to it. Finally that caught on—and the better the opening slots on tours became for us, the better the response was, and the more people we reached. Finally, it all just turned over."

Touring can be very rewarding, but it takes a lot of

planning and hard work to keep the show on the road. As musicians, we have to rely on many competent, trustworthy people to do their jobs consistently if we're going to have a successful tour. Assembling the right road personnel is a challenging job. The crucial first step takes place when your management hires a tour manager. This person must know what

IN THE END, THE LIVE SHOW IS WHAT IT'S ALL ABOUT. HERE, THE RED HOT CHILI PEPPERS PERFORM AT LOLLAPALOOZA.

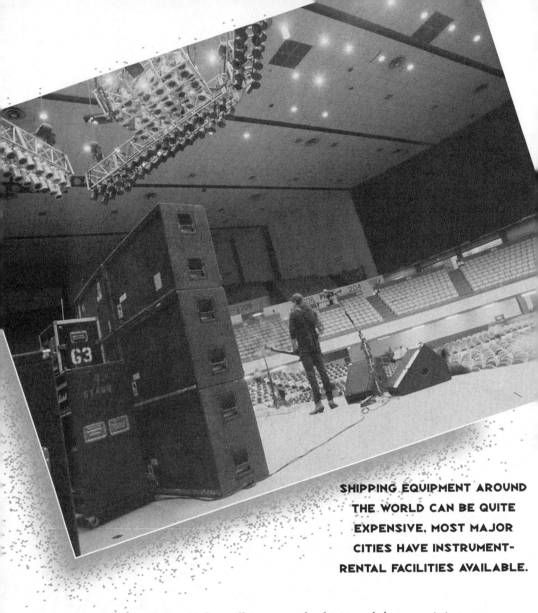

SHIPPING EQUIPMENT AROUND THE WORLD CAN BE QUITE EXPENSIVE. MOST MAJOR CITIES HAVE INSTRUMENT-RENTAL FACILITIES AVAILABLE.

he's doing, because he will oversee the hiring of the remaining crew and supervise the entire operation.

Teamwork is essential to keep everything running smoothly. Aside from traveling together in cramped confines on vans or tour buses, sharing hotel rooms, and working closely with each other at concert venues, the crew often spends months on the road away from their families and homes. The task becomes even more difficult on a tight budget that precludes even a reasonable level of comfort. For this reason, everyone must be able, to some extent, to separate their personal lives from business in order to stay sane. This includes the musicians!

Before you can begin a tour, the budget must be prepared. This is the only accurate way to determine the profit or loss factor. If there are financial problems at this stage, strategies can be implemented to overcome them. Although the preparation of these budgets is the responsibility of the tour manager and/or business manager, the ultimate financial responsibility for success resides with the artist—so it's a good idea to be aware of how your tour budget works.

Most musicians, myself included, enjoy the comforts of a properly staffed tour. This is fine if the budget allows it. If not, there are several ways to cut spending; these include lowering salaries (including the band's), sharing backline personnel, forgoing top-notch hotels, and even spending some nights on the bus from time to time. Most artists choose to lease, rather than purchase, their sound and light systems, staging, buses, and trucks, since these are very expensive items to own and maintain.

This brings to mind some considerations regarding transportation. In North America, bus drivers must be compensated for their overtime, which is anything over 500 miles of continuous driving time. In Europe, the vehicles have a meter in the dashboard that monitors the hours and miles driven; European drivers legally cannot drive for more than eight continuous hours, with a required rest break after four hours. Border patrols check these meters to insure everyone's safety. I mention this because driving long distances not only takes time but can become costly if the distance between venues is too great. Hopefully, your booking agent will keep this in mind when routing your tours!

Shipping equipment around the world can be quite expensive, and a good rule of thumb is: "When in doubt, leave it out." This includes heavy, bulky items such as wardrobe trunks, speaker cabinets, and drum sets. Most major cities have instrument-rental facilities available, and the money spent on rentals is usually less than the cost of shipping gear overseas. Most of the time, your audience will never know if you're playing with hired gear.

The governments of any foreign countries where you may play will insist upon a valid passport and a work visa for every working member of the tour. Work visas must be obtained in order to enter and depart countries where money is earned from a performance. It's usually the responsibility of the tour manager to apply for these visas. Each person is responsible for his own passport. If you don't have one, application forms are available at your local post office, city hall, or library. To apply, you will need two passport-size photographs (obtainable at most photo shops), a birth certificate, and money for the application fee. Make sure you apply for a passport well in advance of any overseas travel, as it usually takes six weeks for processing.

To help give you an overview of the entire operation, I've compiled a list of the working personnel for a major tour. (All of these positions may not be necessary for smaller-scale tours.) The chain of command is as follows:

Tour Manager. On the road, he's the top dog. The tour manager is charged with carrying out the tasks specified by the artist's management and seeing that everything works smoothly. He always accompanies the tour; in most cases, he travels with the band.

Tour Accountant. It's his job to settle the finances for each show and account for merchandise sales on the night of the performance. He's the traveling banker as well, paying per diems (daily expense allowances), hotel bills, and other expenses. On a tighter budget, the tour manager usually handles this job.

Production Manager. He must see to it that the show is up and running every night. The production manager supervises the crew and any local stagehands that are hired. He's also responsible for planning the production requirements for upcoming performances, so he's usually thinking about

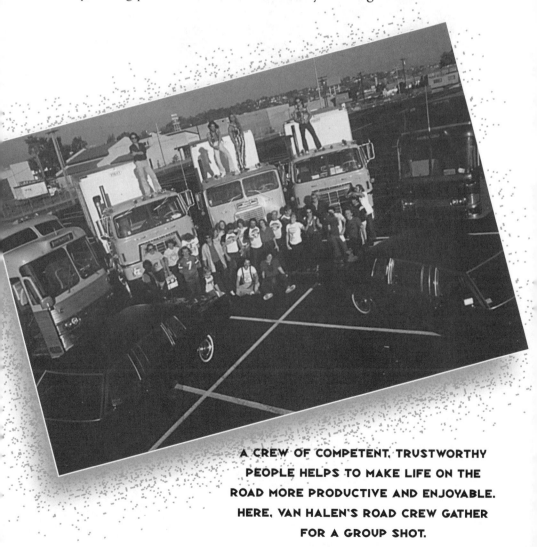

A CREW OF COMPETENT, TRUSTWORTHY PEOPLE HELPS TO MAKE LIFE ON THE ROAD MORE PRODUCTIVE AND ENJOYABLE. HERE, VAN HALEN'S ROAD CREW GATHER FOR A GROUP SHOT.

Photo by Ebet Roberts

tomorrow's show while he works on today's. His day starts when the trucks arrive at the venue to unload the gear, and it finishes late at night, when the final truck is loaded and ready to head to the next town.

Lighting Director. LD's, as they are commonly known, operate the stage lighting system. Some of them are also lighting designers who design the system and plan its use in the show.

Spotlight Operators. These technicians take instructions from the LD as to the color and positioning of the spotlights they operate.

Front-of-House Sound Engineer. He mixes the sound and operates the main PA system, which is what the audience hears.

Monitor Sound Engineer. He mixes the sound and operates the gear for the onstage sound system, which is what the musicians hear.

Backline and Instrument Technicians. There are usually several of these people on the crew. Their responsibilities include stringing and tuning guitars, assembling and tuning drums, and setting up amplifiers. They also repair and maintain the instruments and amplifiers.

Wardrobe. When the budget allows, there's usually one person responsible for maintaining the artists' stage wardrobes.

Electricians. Electricians handle the wiring and maintenance of all the electrical equipment.

Riggers & Carpenters. The riggers figure out how to hang all the lighting and sound equipment. Carpenters construct stage sets and barricades.

Steel Crew. For large outdoor events, a steel crew is needed to erect the giant scaffolding that houses the stage and PA.

Truck and Bus Drivers. They get the band, the crew, and the gear to each destination.

Obviously, the bigger the budget a band has, the more road personnel they can bring with them. For instance, a production manager can tend to many of the ongoing production details while the tour manager or accountant settles the show's finances. If the budget does not allow for hiring all of these people, you may have to handle some of the tasks yourself, just as you did when you played in local clubs.

MONDAY, JULY 24
DEER CREEK MUSIC CENTER

INDIANAPOLIS, IN
EASTERN TIME

TRAVEL

> **BAND**   DRIVE TO INDIANAPOLIS - 215 MILES (4. 5 HRS)
>
> **CREW**   IN INDIANAPOLIS

HOTEL

BAND (IN AM 7/25)	**CREW**
HOLIDAY INN	NO HOTEL
120 WEST BROADWAY	
LOUISVILLE, KY 40202	

TEL 502/555-2241
FAX 502/555-8591
CTC TAMMY

RM SERVICE 6:00 AM - 11:00 PM
TO VENUE 5 BLOCKS

VENUE

DEER CREEK MUSIC CENTER	**CAPACITY**
12880 EAST 146TH STREET	20,118
NOBLESVILLE, IN 46060	

TEL 317/555-8900

SOUND CHECK TBA
DOORS 5:00 PM
SHOWTIME 6:30 PM

PROMOTER SANDCREEK PARTNERS

TEL 317/555-8900
FAX 317/555-7843
CTC DAVE LUCAS

AFTER SHOW TRAVEL

> **BAND** ⎤
>   ⎬ DRIVE TO LOUISVILLE - 115 MILES (2.5 HRS)
> **CREW** ⎦

SUNDAY, AUGUST 13
COMPTON TERRACE

PHOENIX, AZ
PACIFIC TIME

TRAVEL

    BAND   CHECK OUT OF HOTEL EN ROUTE TO VENUE

    CREW   IN PHOENIX

HOTEL

BAND	**CREW**
EMBASSY SUITES	NO HOTEL
1515 N. 44TH STREET	
PHOENIX, AZ 85008	

    TEL 602/555-8800
    FAX 602/555-8800
    CTC JANEAN

TO VENUE 15 MILES

VENUE

COMPTON TERRACE   **CAPACITY**
20000 S. MARICOPA PLACE   22,000
CHANDLER, AZ 85281

TEL 602/555-0240   **SOUND CHECK** TBA
                     DOORS 5:30 PM
               SHOWTIME 7:00 PM

PROMOTER EVENING STAR PRODUCTIONS

    TEL 602/555-6161
    FAX 602/555-0264
    CTC DANNY ZELISKO / TER

AFTER SHOW TRAVEL

    BAND
           } DRIVE TO SAN ANTONIO - 985 MILES (19.5 HRS)
    CREW

Photo by Ebet Roberts

We started from scratch and created a unique sound that was our own thing. We put flyers on light poles and played clubs in New York as often as possible, handling everything ourselves. Self-promotion is hard work. We signed with a small label, Sire Records, because we felt they understood us. We became the band that gave the label an identity.

In the Ramones, you had to hold up your end and be responsible. We were a team—a brotherhood—and we had a strong vision about what we were doing. We grew up on the three-minute song, and we always felt strongly about integrity and quality. If someone started to get a swelled head, we'd knock him down. In the early days, we set down rules for ourselves; for instance, we always played sober. Kids work hard to make money to see a show, and we knew they wanted to see an exciting show, not a bunch of drunks. You want to be at your best when you're up there.

—Joey Ramone

LEAD SINGER FOR THE RAMONES

CONCERT PROMOTERS

OF ALL THE JOBS IN THE MUSIC BUSINESS, THAT OF CONCERT promoter has got to be one of the toughest. Promoting concerts is a financial gamble, and the margin for profits can be very thin, especially with new acts.

Concert promoters are key players in the live-performance business, and there are promoters at all levels, from the ones who book talent for local nightclubs all the way up to those who stage concerts in arenas and stadiums. There are some exceptional promoters who do a fine job of booking, advertising, and handling every detail for concert engagements. There are also some real bottom-feeders who slime around and cut corners wherever possible. With these guys, ticket sales may lag due to inadequate advertising. Or poor security can cause hassles for the tour staff as well as making it unsafe for the audience. Or the artist may be charged back for mysterious "unauthorized" expenses. For these reasons, I'm always grateful to play for a promoter who knows exactly what he's doing and works hard to insure a smooth event.

Your booking agent should handle the particulars of all concert engagements, and he should know how to weed out the bad seeds among the concert promoters. If you don't have an agent, there are a few essentials that should be in order before you hit the concert trail. First and foremost, always have signed contracts stating the exact terms and conditions

CONCERT PROMOTERS ARE KEY PLAYERS IN THE LIVE-PERFORMANCE BUSINESS. PICTURED HERE: SEBASTIAN BACH OF SKID ROW BASKS IN THE AFTER-GLOW OF A WELL-RECEIVED PERFORMANCE.

of each performance. These include the show date, venue name and address, length of performance, other acts on the bill, and—most important—the financial guarantee. The standard payment agreement is 50 percent of the guarantee from the promoter in advance as a deposit for the show; the remainder is collected on the day of the show, following the performance.

It may be necessary to specify production details, such as sound and light requirements, dressing room availability, equipment load-in time, local curfews, and any union rules that may apply. A rider can be attached to the contract that includes artist requests such as food, drinks, towels, etc. (A sample of a standard rider is shown in the Appendix, page 137.) Whatever the terms, everything will work much more efficiently if the show is handled by a top-notch concert promoter.

WORKING WITH A GOOD CONCERT PROMOTER IS A KEY TO THE SUCCESS OF YOUR LIVE PERFORMANCES.

RAVELER'S TIPS

FOR MANY MUSICIANS, TRAVELING BECOMES A WAY OF life. As I've said before, behind all the excitement is a lifestyle that's very demanding and requires a lot of hard work. It's also one that can be downright confusing if you're unfamiliar with the local customs and currencies in foreign countries.

When I was a teenager, I was entertained by stories of rock stars trashing hotel rooms. It just seemed like one big party. That fantasy disappeared quickly when I learned they had to pay for this reckless "fun" with their own hard-earned money. Needless to say, destroying televisions and mattresses is a hefty and unnecessary tour expense!

Many of us make our home for nights on end in hotels and motels, and it pays to be welcome there. Disruptive behavior is a surefire method of getting your entire entourage banned from most hotel chains. This holds true with the hospitality business in general—restaurants, rental-car services, airlines, etc. We rely on these institutions and services to make our traveling more comfortable, so it's a good idea not to alienate them.

When you're staying in a hotel, the tour manager generally covers the room and tax charges for the entourage as part of the group's touring expense. Bear in mind that this is *your* money being spent. It's the responsibility of each individual to pay his own incidentals, which includes such charges as in-room mini-bars, room service, restaurant charges, and laundry. That's why a daily allowance, called a per diem, is issued to all tour personnel.

In the United States, the standard gratuity rate is 15 to 20 percent. General practice is a 15 percent tip for service; this is increased to 20 percent when the service is exceptional. Use

Photo by Ebet Roberts

FOR MANY MUSICIANS, TRAVELING BECOMES A WAY OF LIFE. PICTURED HERE, TOM PETTY BACKSTAGE.

IF YOU TRAVEL A LOT, YOUR REPUTATION FROM THE LAST TRIP PRECEDES YOU. REMEMBER: "WHEN IN ROME . . . ." HERE, MEMBERS OF VAN HALEN AWAIT THE NEXT STAGE OF THEIR JOURNEY.

your own judgment. Tips abroad can be a whole different ball game. In some European countries, tipping is not customary—and in some cultures, it's an insult! Sometimes, gratuities are already added into the bill; this is common with meal service in some countries, so be sure to find out. When you're in a country you've never visited before, always consult with your travel agent and the hotel concierge regarding local customs.

If you need to exchange your U.S. dollars for the local currency, the most convenient place to do this is with the hotel cashier. The exchange rate will probably not be as good as it is at the local banks, but the convenience factor may outweigh the savings. It's best to exchange money in small amounts to avoid being stuck with currency you may no longer need. Each time you exchange to another currency, you'll most likely take a loss. Once you've returned home, it may be difficult to exchange your leftover foreign currency—and its value will be diminished. Lack of planning in this area has helped me to accumulate quite a collection of odd (and useless) money from around the world.

If you travel a lot, you may deal with the same people repeatedly—and you will be preceded by your reputation from the last trip. Remember: "When in Rome . . . ."

Just for kicks, I'll share with you some of my personal travel quirks:

RESTAURANTS

1. Daily specials and "blackened" dishes are usually foods that are about to go bad.
2. The "soup du jour" may be leftover side dishes and entrees from the day before mixed together.
3. Whining about your food can be dangerous. Be cautious about sending a meal back to the chef. No explanation needed!
4. The waiters and chefs are handling your food, so be kind and tip well!
5. Remember that restaurants may recycle items such as bread, rolls, and garnishes.

HOTELS

1. If you'd like your postcard to arrive at its destination, stamp and mail it yourself.
2. Avoid using the in-room mini-bars whenever possible. They certainly aren't cheap.
3. Be prepared to tip for hotel services provided by the bell-men and concierge. Keep a few singles handy for these occasions.
4. Collect airline mileage and hotel bonus points upon checkout, whenever possible. Room upgrades are some-times available by enrolling in hotel travel-award programs.

TRAVEL

1. Avoid having to pick up your airline tickets at the airport ticket counter.
2. When renting automobiles, decline the optional insurance and damage waivers if you already have coverage from a major credit card and adequate auto insurance. (If you're not sure, find out.)
3. Present your frequent-flyer card at the airport gate to ensure you will receive the mileage for your flight. Even if your travel agent has previously entered your account number, it can't hurt to double-check.

IF YOU SPEND A LOT OF TIME ON THE ROAD, IT PAYS TO BE COURTEOUS WITH THE HOSPITALITY INDUSTRY IN ORDER TO BE WELCOMED BACK.

Alot of the people who buy records don't realize what goes into a band's career. When Guns N' Roses started, I was very naïve. I didn't have any aspirations about where I wanted it to go; I was focused on just playing. But every single day, there are things to pick up and new experiences that happen—if you pay attention, you learn from them. Our whole career has been a learning process.

—Slash

GUITARIST FOR GUNS N' ROSES

PART
FIVE

GEAR & MORE

ERCHANDISE DEALS

A MERCHANDISE DEAL CAN PAY LARGER DIVIDENDS than recording or publishing royalties, especially for artists who tour a lot. Here's how it works: A license deal is made between the artist and a merchandise company to market such items as shirts, hats, stickers, and pins that bear the artist's name, logo, or likeness; these items are sold at concerts and in stores. (And if there's one style of music that seems to lend itself well to merchandising, it's heavy metal. Metal bands account for a large amount of the merchandise sold each year, and the audiences at shows are usually decked out in clothes featuring the name or symbol of the band.)

My Megadeth bandmate Dave Mustaine notes that it's very important for the artwork to be catchy. In the case of a T-shirt, Dave says, "There must be a signature icon, character, or piece of artwork that's distinctive, so if people see only four to six inches of it, they will still be able to instantly recognize what it is." (In addition to being the singer/guitarist for Megadeth, Dave has successfully launched two clothing companies, Ded Threads and Melting Pot International, Inc.)

For the convenience of artists who have not yet developed satisfactory artwork, most merchandisers offer the services of a graphic artist. To insure the highest level of

MERCHANDISE DEALS INCLUDE BOTH
RETAIL AND LIVE-PERFORMANCE
SALES, AND THEY USUALLY OFFER
ADVANCES AGAINST FUTURE
ROYALTIES. PICTURED HERE: DAVID
ELLEFSON WITH MEGADETH ITEMS.

LIVE-PERFORMANCE AND
MERCHANDISING ROYALTIES ARE
BASED ON GROSS SALES AND
CALCULATED ON A PER-HEAD
BASIS. HERE, THE SMASHING
PUMPKINS PACK 'EM IN.

artistic integrity, there should be a stipulation in the contract that gives the artist final approval of any and all
artwork. The merchandiser will then market this artwork
in as many ways possible, for everyone's benefit.

Merchandise deals include both retail and live-performance sales, and they usually offer advances against
future royalties. The retail portion of the deal covers
sales to record stores, T-shirt shops, and other retail outlets. These royalties are based on net sales—that is, the
wholesale price of the merchandise. The amount of the
advance is based on the artist's prior sales record or the
merchandiser's projection of future sales.

Live-performance royalties, on the other hand, are
based on gross sales and calculated on a per-head basis.
This means the gross sales figure is divided by the
number of concert attendees. Here's an example of how
it's done:

Gross sales figure	$10,000
Show attendance	1,000
Per-head calculation	$10
Artist receives 40 percent royalty:	$10 X 40% = $ 4 per head
Total royalty =	$4,000

Merchandisers base live-performance advances on
the size of a tour and the estimated attendance at each
show. This may put the artist in the unfortunate position
of having to pay back any unrecouped portion of an
advance if sales fall short of the merchandiser's
projection. For this reason, usually only a portion of the
live-performance advance is paid before the start of a

tour. The remaining installments are then paid once the tour is successfully in progress. Holding out for an outrageous advance is not always the shrewdest business decision with regard to merchandise deals. It's better to take a small advance and be sure you won't be left holding the bag.

FOR SOME ARTISTS, MERCHANDISE CAN BE THEIR MOST LUCRATIVE SOURCE OF INCOME.

EQUIPMENT ENDORSEMENTS

WHEN AN ARTIST ENDORSES A MUSICAL PRODUCT, HE acknowledges to the world his equipment preference and gives it his seal of approval. Endorsements are a two-way street, and they can be quite beneficial for promoting both the artist and the manufacturer. Equipment manufacturers receive widespread exposure when well-known musicians perform with their products and are seen with them in photographs. Artists, on the other hand, receive gear for free or at a vastly reduced price, and they get the extra publicity that comes with appearing in advertisements.

Let's take a look at two different types of endorsement deals. The first is the *exclusive* endorsement agreement. In this type of deal, the artist agrees to endorse only one company's product of a particular type. The manufacturer expects the artist to use its product onstage and appear in advertisements. This does not necessarily mean that he can't ever play another instrument; it simply restricts him from endorsing a competitor's product. In return for this exclusivity, the artist receives free equipment and possibly other considerations, such as loaner gear for recording and live per-formances. Many of the larger manufacturers have ample budgets allowing for more than just advertising, and some sponsor appearances by their endorsees at trade shows and clinics to demonstrate the use of their equipment.

WHEN AN ARTIST ENDORSES A MUSICAL PRODUCT, HE ACKNOWLEDGES TO THE WORLD HIS EQUIPMENT PREFERENCE. PICTURED HERE: DAVID ELLEFSON ENDORSES D'ADDARIO STRINGS. PAINTING BY JOHN RAFFERTY.

A *non-exclusive* endorsement allows an artist to be a spokesperson for a product without imposing any restrictions. In this case, the artist is free to use whatever other equipment he chooses in live performances and photographs without violating the endorsement agreement. But he may have to purchase gear at a wholesale price rather than receive it free, and his exposure in advertising campaigns may be less than what it would be if he were an exclusive endorser.

One artist who believes in an honest endorsement policy is bassist Billy Sheehan, who's well known for his work with Talas, David Lee Roth, and Mr. Big. "If I endorse something," says Billy, "it's important for me to know that the kid who sees the ad in a magazine and goes out and buys the product is not getting a stroke from me. I use what I say I use, and stick with that product for a long time."

Ken Hensley was the keyboardist in the band Uriah Heep, and today he handles artist relations for St. Louis Music, the company that manufactures and distributes Ampeg, Crate, and Alvarez equipment. Ken has seen both sides of the situation, and he offers this thought about endorsements: "Professional artist endorsements are an investment of the company's money, product, manpower, and general expenses, and they have proven to work as part of the overall marketing scheme. We're looking for promotion and visibility. Real-life use of the product is one of the most important aspects of the endorsement relationship."

When a manufacturer maintains a disposition such as this toward endorsements, it can be a win-win situation for both the artist and the company. Some companies even offer lucrative deals to artists in return for the use of their equipment—in other words, there may be situations where you can actually be *paid* to use certain gear. You should carefully consider these commitments, though. I believe it's best to choose the equipment you use on its true merit, not just because of the money or advertising. Both you and the manufacturer will be better served when you endorse a product you're truly proud to use. Ultimately this is a matter of personal integrity, and something you must decide for yourself.

EQUIPMENT ENDORSEMENTS CAN BE BENEFICIAL TO BOTH YOU AND THE MANUFACTURER—BUT CONSIDER THESE COMMITMENTS CAREFULLY.

A lot of people think you have to have a grand plan that's been worked out upfront and then taken to completion—but in actuality, things just happen! The ability to adapt to changing times, changing styles of music, and the people you work with is really valuable. The ability to make good decisions is important, too, and you sometimes have to make the most critical decisions in the worst possible situations. When the world is caving in around you, you must be at your best. I try to get as much information as possible before making a decision, rather than making a compulsive move. Anything above a 50 percent success rate puts you ahead of the game!

—*Billy* Sheehan
BASSIST FOR MR. BIG

COPYRIGHT, OWNERSHIP, AND INCORPORATION

AS YOU MAY KNOW, THERE ARE LAWS TO PROTECT what is known as intellectual property. These laws are vital to your success in the music business, and I'd like to take just a minute to discuss some key aspects of copyright and ownership.

In the "Music Publishing" section (page 59), I mentioned that one of the advantages of having a music publisher is that the publisher will secure copyrights for your songs. But what if you don't have a music publisher? Well, you can obtain the official forms from the Library of Congress and copyright the songs yourself. There's also a great package available from Valco Graphics called *The Copyright Kit,* which includes the necessary forms; this is available at many music stores.

Anytime you identify yourself professionally with a name, you need to secure a trademark for that as well. If you're in a band, this is very important—a trademark will protect you should anyone decide to infringe on the use of your name. Overlooking this crucial step can not only be annoying but damaging, especially if you've developed a loyal following.

To secure a trademark for your name, you'll need to hire an attorney who specializes in this work. He will run a worldwide check on the name to determine if it's

ANYTIME YOU IDENTIFY YOURSELF
PROFESSIONALLY WITH A NAME,
YOU NEED TO SECURE A
TRADEMARK FOR IT. PICTURED
HERE: AEROSMITH, A BAND THAT
HAS LONG BEEN
IDENTIFIABLE BY ITS NAME.

Circular **56**

Copyright for
Sound
Recordings

Circular **50**

Copyright
Registrat...
for Musica...
Composition...

THE **COPYRIGHT**™ KIT

EVERYTHING YOU NEED TO
COPYRIGHT YOUR SONGS
WHETHER YOUR MUSIC IS WRITTEN OR RECORDED

This Kit Includes:
• 2 Instruction Booklets
• 12 Forms
• 6 Envelopes
• 6 Labels

THE LAWS TO PROTECT INTEL-
LECTUAL PROPERTY ARE VITAL
TO YOUR SUCCESS IN THE
MUSIC BUSINESS.

available; if someone else has already trademarked it, you'll probably need to choose a different name. After the name has cleared, the attorney will file for ownership. If you're in a group, you must decide if one or all members will acquire ownership. This is an important decision—bear in mind that a single owner may be legally entitled to use of the name without any of the other members. (This has happened more than once in the music business!) Ownership of a name doesn't necessarily dictate how the earnings will be split. As I mentioned earlier, there are many ways to divide the money that a group earns. Some groups prefer to divide everything equally, while others use more complicated methods.

At this point, let's discuss the shared expenses that offset your earnings. There will always be ongoing costs to operate a group; this is known as *overhead*, and everyone should be in agreement as to how the overhead will be covered. Even if the group disbands, someone will be responsible for the outstanding financial obligations. This point should be discussed early on, and every-one ought to be clear about how expenses will be handled.

This raises an important question: Should your group go into business as a partnership or a corporation? In a partnership, the partners may be personally responsible to pay the group's debts. But if you form a corporation, the individual members will not be individually responsible. Forming a corporation offers additional advantages, including sophisticated tax structuring, pension plans, and insurance benefits. Consult your business manager and attorney for direction in this area.

Success has a way of changing a person's perspective

in many ways—especially when large amounts of money are involved. Along the way, some people become belligerent about what constitutes their fair share. Making important business decisions early can help you to avoid confusion and lawsuits at a later date.

IF YOU MAKE THE RIGHT DECISIONS ABOUT COPYRIGHT, OWNERSHIP, AND INCORPORATION EARLY IN YOUR CAREER, YOU WILL BE PROTECTED FROM THE FINANCIAL HASSLES THAT CAN ACCOMPANY SUCCESS.

THE ART OF NEGOTIATING

TO GET WHAT YOU NEED TO ADVANCE YOUR CAREER, YOU must know how to negotiate. As they say in the real-estate business, "Everything is negotiable," and you will discover that as your musical career develops you will be involved in negotiations with your bandmates, management, record labels, promoters, and many of the other people I've mentioned in this book. Airline magazines often feature ads where high-powered executives claim: "In business you don't get what you deserve, but what you negotiate." That's true. In my opinion, the most successful negotiations produce a win-win situation for all parties involved—this means that everyone gets a fair deal.

A wise negotiator is realistic about his worth and has his facts straight. There are many shrewd people in the music business, and the only way to survive is to know where you stand before you head to the negotiating table. Too often, artists become arrogant and shoot themselves in the foot by being stubborn and unrealistic.

It's important to separate your needs from your wants. This is not to say you won't ever get what you want, but it's important to focus on what you really need. One of the basic principles of deal-making is compromise—you must know when to give a little in order to get something in return. Prioritizing the points of a deal will help you to distinguish the less consequential items from the more important ones.

Whenever you negotiate, be sure you're prepared and have some knowledge of the people with whom you are negotiating. I was once given a great piece of advice: "Don't make business decisions based on emotion." Keeping your focus on the facts will help to prevent emotional and irrational thinking in heated negotiations. By doing this, you stand a much better chance of making sound decisions and creating the desired win-win outcome.

DEVELOPING NEGOTIATING SKILLS TAKES TIME AND PRACTICE, JUST AS LEARNING TO MASTER A MUSICAL INSTRUMENT DOES. THE MORE YOU DO IT, THE MORE CONFIDENT YOU WILL BECOME.

I have never involved myself in any way with the business side of things. I've always entrusted all business considerations to my manager, accountant, lawyer, agent, and road crew. My advice would be: Get someone else to do the business!

—Chrissie Hynde

LEAD SINGER/GUITARIST FOR THE PRETENDERS

PART SIX

IN CLOSING

THE IMPORTANCE OF ATTITUDE

WE'VE ALL HEARD THE EXPRESSION "ATTITUDE IS everything." The *American Heritage Dictionary* defines attitude as "a state of mind or feeling with regard to a person or thing." The further I travel down the road of life, the more I realize how the outcome of any situation can be seriously affected by my attitude toward it.

How does attitude apply to an artist? As a performance tool, many successful entertainers use their "attitude" as part of their onstage image. That's not what I mean—I'm talking about the way you handle yourself offstage, especially in your dealings with the business world. You should always be aware of the manner in which you conduct yourself and the degree of consideration you show to your associates. Never forget that the level of respect you receive is often proportional to the level of respect you show to others.

The most successful people you'll ever meet have, at some point in their careers, had to dig deep within themselves to bring forth a positive attitude to overcome obstacles they faced. Often, it's simply a matter of swallowing your pride. More artists have been destroyed by their all-consuming egos and lack of consideration for their peers than anything else. Bear in mind that an artist's career doesn't last forever—when the curtain finally closes, you can either walk away with your dignity intact or suffer a long, hard fall from grace. Being honorable and humble on the way up can help you a lot when the chips are down.

In the music business, people often bounce from one gig to another. This is yet another reason to be respectful toward people. You never know if the "small people" you meet today will become the powerful and influential forces of tomorrow.

Many people think nice guys finish last—but in my experience, the opposite holds true. The future is uncertain. If you're out there burning bridges, you'll surely regret it later when you can't get to the other side.

HONOR AND HUMILITY CAN BE GREAT ASSETS. MORE ARTISTS HAVE BEEN DESTROYED BY THEIR ALL-CONSUMING EGOS AND LACK OF CONSIDERATION FOR THEIR PEERS THAN ANYTHING ELSE.

# FAREWELL

I HOPE YOU'VE FOUND THE INFORMATION ON THESE pages helpful and even beneficial. I've tried to touch on many topics that you will encounter as you pursue your career. Too often, novice musicians lack the essential knowledge of business that's required for survival in the music industry. As a result, they get discouraged or find themselves in compromising situations.

I think it's important to realize that every person's musical path is unique. Sometimes we try to model ourselves after others, usually our influences and idols. Often we're disappointed with the outcome, though, because we all have to find our own way.

I made this discovery when I moved from rural Minnesota to Los Angeles in 1983. I arrived with my dreams in tow and stood alone on a Hollywood street corner, scared to death of what was to become of me. I knew I had only two choices: return to my hometown with my tail between my legs, or dive right in and learn how to play the game with the best of 'em. There have certainly been low points in my career when I thought it would be best to spare myself the torment and just throw in the towel. Fortunately, I stuck it out—and I've never regretted it.

Playing music for a living has been a dream come true for me, and I can't emphasize enough how important it is to take some risks in order to pursue *your* lifelong dreams. You will no doubt encounter setbacks along the way, and your dreams may be all you'll have. But I encourage you to give it your best shot and—most of all—keep your passion for music alive.

Best of luck!

PPENDIX

RECOMMENDED READING

If you'd like to learn more about the music business, I recommend the following books:

All You Need to Know About the Music Business, by Donald Passman, Simon & Schuster.

This Business of Music, edited by M. William Krasilovsky & Sidney Shemel, Billboard Books.

The Art of Music Licensing, by Al Kohn & Bob Kohn, Aspen Law.

The Yellow Pages of Rock, Album Network.

RIDER

Here's a sample of a standard artist rider for concert appearances. For more samples contracts and detailed explanations of their provisions, refer to one of the books listed on the previous page.

This rider attached hereto and made part of the contract dated _____ by and between CORPORATION (hereinafter referred to as "Producer") furnishing the services of CLIENT (hereinafter referred to as "Artist") and _____ (hereinafter referred to as "Purchaser").

1. BILLING

Artist shall receive 100% Sole Star Billing in any and all publicity releases and paid advertisements, including but not limited to programs, fliers, signs, lobby boards and marquees. No other name or photograph shall appear in type with respect to size, thickness, boldness and prominence of the type accorded Artist and no other name or photograph shall appear on the same line or above the name of Artist.

2. CANCELLATION

Purchaser agrees that Artist may cancel the engagement hereunder, at Artist's sole discretion, by giving Purchaser notice thereof at least thirty (30) days prior to the commencement date of the engagement hereunder.

3. FORCE MAJEURE

Producer's obligation to furnish the entertainment unit referred to herein is subject to the detention or prevention by sickness, inability to perform, accident, means of transportation, Act of God, riots, strikes, labor difficulties, epidemics and any act or order of any public authority or any cause, similar or dissimilar, beyond Producer's control.

Provided Artist is ready, willing and able to perform, Purchaser agrees to compensate Producer in accordance with the terms hereof regardless of Act of God, fire, accident, riot , strike or any events of any kind or character whatsoever, whether similar or dissimilar to the foregoing events which would prevent or interfere with the presentation of the show hereunder.

4. INCLEMENT WEATHER

Notwithstanding anything contained herein, inclement weather shall not be deemed to be a force majeure occurrence and the Purchaser shall remain liable for payment of the full contract price even if the performance(s) called for herein are prevented by such weather conditions. Producer shall have the sole right to determine in good faith whether any such weather conditions shall render the performance(s) impossible, hazardous or unsafe.

5. CONTROL OF PRODUCTION

Producer shall have the sole and exclusive control over the production, presentation and performance of the entertainment unit in connection with the engagement, including but not limited to, the details, means and methods of the performance of the entertainment unit and each member thereof, and the persons to be employed by Producer in performing the provisions hereof on Artist's part to be performed. Producer shall have the sole right, as Producer may see fit, to designate and change the performing personnel other than artist. It is specifically understood and agreed that a representative of the Producer shall have sole and absolute authority in directing personnel operating all lighting and sound equipment during rehearsal and each performance scheduled herein.

6. APPROVAL OF OTHER PERFORMERS
Producer reserves the approval right of any other persons to appear in conjunction with this performance and the right to determine the length and nature of their performance(s). A violation of this clause shall entitle Producer to refuse to furnish the performers described herein but Purchaser shall remain obligated to make all payments herein set forth. Purchaser agrees that there will be no Master of Ceremonies, no welcoming speeches, no introductions, and no ceremonies at intermission except as Producer may direct.

7. REPRODUCTION OF PERFORMANCE
No portion of the performance rendered hereunder may be broadcast, photographed, recorded, filmed, taped or embodied in any form for any purpose or reproducing such performance without Producer's prior written consent. Purchaser will deny entrance to any persons carrying audio or video recording devices without limiting in any way the generality of the foregoing prohibition, it is understood to include members of the audience, press and Purchaser's staff.

In the event that the Purchaser, his agents, servants, employees, contractors, etc., reproduce or cause to be reproduced the Producer's performance in the form of films, tapes, or any other means of audio or video reproductions, upon demand by Artist, Purchaser shall deliver all of the same (together with any and all masters, negatives and other means of reproductions thereof) to Producer at Purchaser's sole cost and expense, in addition to all other legal or equitable remedies which Producer may have.

8. PURCHASER ASSUMES LIABILITY
Except as otherwise herein specifically provided, Purchaser hereby assumes full liability and responsibility for the payment of any and all cost, expenses, charges, claims, losses, liabilities, and damages related to or based upon the presentation or production of the show or shows in which Artist is to appear hereunder.

9. SPONSORSHIP
All forms of sponsorship, whether part of an ongoing series or specifically for Artist's show, must be authorized by Producer.

10. BOX OFFICE PROVISIONS
In cases where the Artist is being paid on a percentage basis, Purchaser agrees to deliver to the Artist's representative, at least two (2) weeks prior to date of performance, a plot plan and printer's manifest of the house (notarized, signed statement from the printer of tickets, listing amount of tickets printed at each price). Purchaser further agrees to have on hand at the place of performance the night of the show, for counting and verification by representative of the Producer, all unsold tickets. Producer shall be compensated for the difference between the number of unsold tickets on hand and shown to its representative and the number of tickets printed as shown by the ticket manifest. If Purchaser shall violate any of the preceding provisions of the paragraph, it shall be deemed that Purchaser has sold a ticket for each seat in the house (and any permitted standing room) at the highest ticket price for which the house is scaled. Purchaser further agrees to give said representative the right to enter the box-office at any time (during and after the performance) and to examine and make extracts from the box-office records of Purchaser relating to the gross receipts of this engagement. A written box-office statement, certified and signed by the Purchaser, will be furnished to Artist within two (2) hours following each performance. Purchaser may not sell tickets to performance herein as part of a subscription or other type of series of other concerts, without written consent of Producer. All tickets printed under the manifest shall be of the one stub, one price vari-

ety. There shall be no multiple price tickets printed. Examples of tickets prohibited under this agreement are:

> a) one price for students and a different price for general admissions of the same ticket, or;
> b) one price for tickets bought in advance and a different price for tickets bought at the gate on the same ticket.

Further, no tickets can be sold for seats located to the rear of the stage where the stage and equipment on stage is obstructing normal eye-level viewing of Artist's performance, unless the location of the seat is clearly indicated on the ticket. Tickets sold behind bandstand must be marked "impaired vision" or "behind bandstand."

If Purchaser violates the above agreement, he shall be liable for the total amount of tickets sold at the highest price printed on the ticket. All tickets shall be printed by a bonded ticket house. (Example - Globe Tickets, Arcus-Simplex) or, if the performance is at a college or university, the official printing department of the university or college. Purchaser agrees not to discount tickets or to offer tickets as a premium without first obtaining permission in writing from the Producer. If Purchaser does sell or distribute discount or complimentary tickets without prior approval, or in excess of the number printed, he shall be liable for the full ticket price of each such ticket sold or distributed.

11. COMPLIMENTARY TICKETS

Purchaser agrees to distribute no more than one percent (1%) of the official house seating as complimentary tickets relative to this performance. Further Purchaser must supply a representative of Producer with a statement detailing to whom each complimentary ticket was given. Each complimentary ticket will be issued only as a fully punched ticket. Purchaser agrees to supply proper radio, television and newspaper personnel and their families with complimentary tickets from above-mentioned allotment.

Purchaser agrees that if NO ADMISSION is charged to any part of the audience for engagement hereunder, this condition must be so stated on the face of the attached contract. If, at the engagement, there is evidence that admission was or is being subsequently charged for Artist's performance, Purchaser agrees that Producer must receive 100% of the admission receipts collected.

In addition, Purchaser must provide Producer with twenty (20) complimentary tickets per show within the first ten (10) rows, the unused portion of which may be placed on sale the day of performance with the permission of Producer.

If place of performance is other than a theater and/or cabaret or nightclub, a booth and/or tables comprising of mini-cabaret of six (6) seats to be called "Star's Booth" or "Table" must be available for each performance and if not to be used at said performance will be released by Producer or their representative.

12. SCALING

Purchaser will clearly print the specific capacity, gross potential, and ticket price breakdown. of the facility where Artist is to perform under this agreement on the face of contract that this agreement is attached to.

In the event Producer is to receive a percentage of the gross receipts for this engagement pursuant to the terms hereof, the term "gross receipts" or "gross box-office receipts" or similar phrases, shall mean all box-office receipts computed on the basis of the full retail ticket price for all tickets sold and in no event less that the full retail ticket price for all persons entering the performance with no deductions of any kind, less only federal, state or local admissions taxes and allowable discounts as approved by Producer in writing. The Purchaser agrees to scale the ticket prices for this engagement of guarantee potential gross receipts of no less than $_____.

13. FAILURE TO FULFILL OBLIGATIONS

Each one of the terms and conditions of this contract is of the essence of this agreement and necessary for Artist's full performance hereunder. In the event Purchaser refuses or neglects to provide any of the items herein stated, and/or fails to make any of the payments as provided herein, Producer shall have the right to refuse to perform this contract, shall retain any amounts theretofore paid to Producer by Purchaser, and Purchaser shall remain liable to Producer for the agreed price herein set forth. In addition, if, on or before the date of any scheduled concert, Purchaser has failed, neglected, or refused to perform any contract with any other performer for any earlier engagement, or if the financial standing or credit of Purchaser has been impaired or is in Producer's opinion unsatisfactory, Producer shall have the right to demand the payment of the guaranteed compensation forthwith, Producer shall have the right to cancel this engagement by notices to Purchaser to that effect, and in such event Producer shall retain any amount theretofore paid to Producer by Purchaser.

14. MODIFICATION OF CONTRACT

It is understood and agreed that the contract may not be changed, modified, or altered, except by an instrument in writing, signed in accordance with the laws of the State of California. This contract may not be assigned, or changed, modified, or altered except by an instrument in writing signed by the parties. Nothing in this agreement shall require the performance of any act contrary to the law or to the rules or regulations of any union, guild, or similar body having jurisdiction over services of Artist or over the performances hereunder. Whenever there is any conflict between any provisions of this contract and any law, or any such rule or regulation of any such union, guild or similar body, such law, rule or regulation shall prevail, and this contract shall be modified to the extent necessary to eliminate such conflict. This is the sole and complete agreement between the parties with respect to the engagement. Nothing in this contract shall be construed to constitute the parties as a partnership or joint venture, and Producer shall not be liable in whole or in part for any obligation that may be incurred by Purchaser in carrying out any of the provisions hereof, or otherwise.

15. INDEMNIFICATION

A. Purchaser agrees to indemnify and hold harmless Producer/Artist and its employees, contractors and/or agents from and against any claims, costs (including attorney's fees and court costs), expenses, damages, liabilities, losses or judgments arising out of, or in connection with, any claim, demand or action made by any third party, if such are sustained as a direct or indirect consequence of the Engagement.

B. Purchaser shall also indemnify and hold harmless Producer/Artist and its employees, contractors and/or agents from and against any and all loss, damage and/or destruction occurring to its and/or its employees', contractors', or agents' instruments and equipment at the place of the Engagement, including, but not limited to, damage, loss or destruction caused by Act of God.

16. TAXES

Purchaser shall pay and hold Producer harmless of and from any and all taxes, fees, dues and the like relating to the engagement hereunder and the sums payable to Producer shall be free of such taxes, fees, dues and the like.

17. CHOICE OF LAW/FORUM

This agreement shall be deemed made and entered into in the State of California and shall be governed by all of the laws of such State applicable to agreements wholly to be performed therein.

18. ANTICIPATORY BREACH

If on or before the date of any scheduled performance hereunder, the financial standing or credit of Promoter has been impaired or is unsatisfactory, Producer shall have the right to demand payment forthwith of the guaranteed compensation specified above, and if Promoter fails or refuses to make such payment forthwith, Producer shall then have the right to cancel this agreement. In the event of such cancellation,

Producer shall have no further obligation to Promoter hereunder, and shall retain any monies theretofore paid to Producer by Promoter.

19. INTERNATIONAL TRAVEL

In the event the place of performance is outside the continental limits of the United States, Purchaser agrees to procure, at his sole expense, for Artist and party, the necessary visas, work permits and other documents of any nature whatsoever necessary or usually obtained to enable Artist to render its services hereunder. Also, Purchaser shall be responsible for, and indemnify and hold Producer/Artist harmless from and against, all local, municipal and country or government taxes, fees or levies on all income earned by Producer, or Producer's employees while in the country or countries covered by this contract.

20. INSURANCE

Purchaser agrees to provide comprehensive general liability insurance (including, without limitation, coverage to protect against any and all injury to persons or property as a consequence of the installation and/or operation of the equipment and instruments provided by Producer and/or its employees, contractors and agents). Such liability insurance shall be in the amount required by the venue, but in no event shall have a limit of less than One Million Dollars ($1,000,000.00) combined single limit for bodily injury and property damage. Such insurance shall be in full force and effect at all times Producer/Artist or any of Producer's agents or independent contractors are in place of performance. Producer/Artist and its agent for the Engagement, shall be listed as additionally-named insureds under such insurance and this shall be indicated on the pertinent certificate of insurance. Purchaser also agrees to provide a policy of Workman's Compensation covering all of Purchaser's employees or third-party contractors. Purchaser further agrees to provide full all-risks insurance coverage for all equipment and instruments provided by Producer and/or its employees, contractors and agents against fire, vandalizing, theft, riot, or any other type of act or event causing harm or damage to, or loss of, the instruments and equipment so provided. Certificates of insurance relating to the coverage listed above shall be furnished by Purchaser to Producer at least fourteen (14) days prior to the Engagement. Producer's failure to request or review such insurance certificates shall not affect Producer's rights or Purchaser's obligations hereunder. The Purchaser warrants that he has complete and adequate public liability insurance. This certificate must be produced to the Producer upon request.

21. MERCHANDISING

The Purchaser will provide a well lit secure place to erect a merchandising stall. This shall be in such a position as to be easily visible to the public using the main entrance. This is to be at no cost to the Producer. Purchaser agrees that its arrangement for presenting the engagement provided for herein shall prohibit the sale of souvenir or similar merchandise on the premises in connection with this engagement other than Producer's official merchandise furnished by Producer.

22. PARAGRAPH HEADINGS

Paragraph headings are inserted in this Rider for convenience only and are not to be used in interpreting this Agreement.

AGREED TO AND ACCEPTED:

_____   _____

PURCHASER   CORPORATION
                                          f/s/o CLIENT

ABOUT THE AUTHOR

David Ellefson started playing music at the age of eight years old, and began his professional musical career at the age of thirteen. As the bassist and a mainstay member of the heavy metal rock group MEGADETH, Ellefson has become a seasoned professional in the music business through countless worldwide concert tours, recording sessions, and music videos. Along with the other members of MEGADETH, he has received five Grammy nominations and is actively involved in writing, recording, and performing. Ellefson resides in Arizona with his wife Julie and son Roman, and when not performing with the band, writes "The Real Deal" column for *Bass Player* magazine, keeps the creative fires burning, and enjoys the great outdoors with hiking, biking, and golfing.

PHOTOGRAPHY CREDITS

Jay Blakesberg   9, 18, 26, 46, 50, 52, 58, 64, 66, 69, 70, 73, 74, 76, 82, 91, 114

Pete Cronin   11, 113, back cover

Glen La Ferman   121

Ken Kaminsky   123

Gene Kirkland   front cover, 35, 86

R. Andrew Lepley   57

John Rafferty   118

Ebet Roberts   41, 45, 55, 87, 96, 100, 105

Neil Zlozower   30, 85, 92, 95, 102, 106, 109, 129